THE EYES ARE THE WINDOW TO THE SOUL

To Chuck Smart, my pots and pans mentor,
whose fiery eyes
ignited my passion.

To Dr. Bob, my dentist,
whose joyful eyes
kept me motivated with inspirational books.

Fire Up Your Life!

A Journey to Transformation

by
Donna Hartley

Fire Up Your Life: A Journey to Transformation

By Donna Hartley

1. Body, Mind & Spirit : Spirituality - General 2. Self-Help : Motivational & Inspirational 3. Biography & Autobiography : Personal Memoirs

ISBN: 978-1-935953-12-8

Cover design by Lewis Agrell

Printed in the United States of America

Authority Publishing

11230 Gold Express Dr. #310-413

Gold River, CA 95670

800-877-1097

www.AuthorityPublishing.com

Fire Up Series

In these uncertain times, the human spirit yearns for hope and enlightenment so each of us may survive and thrive. The **Fire Up** series recounts a compelling true-life journey, delivering timely inspiration along with timeless wisdom. Donna Hartley is crowned Miss Hawaii and her attention is captured by a kind and patient soul, George, who mysteriously prophesies that her success is paved with learning lessons. He relates to her in storytelling form that Donna must survive three life-threatening events if she is to fulfill her destiny. Is George a wise man, a mentor, an angel, or all three?

Fire Up Your Life! recounts Donna's near-death experience in a DC-10 plane crash at Los Angeles International Airport, which occurs directly after she expresses her desire to change her life or die. Trapped in the flaming inferno, she receives a mysterious message questioning her actions on earth. She wills herself to survive and is the last passenger out of her section of the aircraft. With the steadfast help of her teacher George, the reluctant student Donna begins a journey of spiritual transformation committing herself to change her fearful and unhealthy lifestyle. Her first assignment is to fight for improved airline safety regulations. Next, she must conquer her destructive relationships with men. Moreover, to become a successful entrepreneur she must master her fears.

Fire Up Your Intuition! finds Donna distraught in an emotional and financial crisis. George unexpectedly appears and bestows on her five mysterious envelopes that hold a 30-day assignment that he calls "the gift of intuition." The banter and discussion continue between student and teacher as Donna works to acquire insight into her own intuitive awareness. Her faithful Himalayan cat Sheba is by her side as Donna follows George's program step by step to learn to trust her feelings and act upon them to master *the knowing*. George predicts that when she completes her assignment, her dream to adopt a daughter will come true.

Fire Up Your Healing! narrates the sometimes rocky path on the passage toward family forgiveness leading to emotional maturity and the strength to heal. Donna travels from the tragic confines of her mother's post-stroke nursing home to the somber quarters of the judge empowered with deciding the fate for the bitter court battle in which her stepmother has embroiled Donna and her brother upon their father's death. George adamantly advises her to release her anger in order to survive. Could she forgive the alcoholism, the violence, and the indifference? This skill is now essential if she is to survive her stage III melanoma. But can she forgive herself and live to raise her six-year-old daughter? George mystically appears in the hospital to give Donna a shot of spiritual adrenalin and the courage to face down the deadly disease.

Fire Up Your Heart! begins at the gravesite of her stepdad as a heartbroken Donna deals with the eleventh death of family and friends in the past few years. Her nagging intuition forces her to consult a heart specialist and the prognosis is her worst fear: she must have immediate open-heart surgery to replace her failing aortic valve. Her daughter Mariah, now age ten, is the driving force to help her live. Donna's friends rally to lend her support for the delicate surgery scheduled for **March 1**, the same date of her plane crash and melanoma diagnosis. What are those chances? Donna must summon all her strength and hard-won wisdom to survive. Will George spiritually guide her through this life-threatening operation? Has Donna learned her lessons so she can cheat death for the third time?

Acknowledgements

To Joan Roelke, who helped me organize this book.

To Pam Vetter, whom I jokingly call my $10,000 friend, and who is priceless for graciously and freely giving her time to help formulate many ideas.

To George, my master teacher, who kept insisting I speak and write.

To Angela Booras, who put her life on hold to offer endless suggestions and countless hours to help finalize this book.

To those who have guided me in body, mind, and spirit with their patience because I had none, and who ignited my firepower.

Table of Contents

Part I
The Crash

Wake-Up Call

"No ... No ... No ... No ..." A bloodcurdling scream woke me ... it was *my* scream! *Can't breathe.* My head jolted off the pillow. Beads of sweat dripped from my hair.

AAAIIIEEE. My hands flew to my ears, pressing harder and harder to block out the screeching noise. "Stop! Stop! Go away ... leave me alone!" *It's the phone. The phone. It's the phone.*

My heart racing, I picked it up. "Hi sweetie, it's Mary Margaret. This is your wake-up call with good wishes for your trip."

Gasping for air, I choked out, "Th-th-thanks."

"Donna, are you all right?"

"It was that dream, the same nightmare I've had before. It was all so real. I'm limping away from a burning aircraft. The flames ... the faces ... the injured people ... the fence."

"Calm down, Donna. Your life hasn't been that great lately, but you're going to Hawaii. The islands have always been good to you. Hey, you were Miss Hawaii."

"You're right. I guess you're right."

"You bet I'm right," Mary Margaret insisted.

"Thank you for calling. Oh, I almost forgot: good luck on your audition today. I have to get going," I said softly.

I willed my body out of bed, all the while mumbling to myself, "A shower, wash away the dreadful dream." The steaming water pounded on my shoulders. My mind was still churning like it was on an endless spin cycle. Suddenly, an uncontrollable primal scream erupted from my throat. "Let my life change! Let it never be the same! Or let me die!"

Chapter One

Love and Accept Yourself

The effort to make a better life
is worth the struggle because the outcome
is a life that serves you

Seat-belted in Continental Flight 603 and speeding down the runway at 167 miles per hour, I felt three massive explosions. Plunged into paralyzing terror as the unthinkable happened, I experienced a jolt so powerful that I felt severed at the waist as my body slammed against the seat belt. Bounced and rocked, surrounded by screeching crashing sounds, an ear-splitting crack met my ears as one wing clipped the tarmac and shattered. The lumbering DC-10 aircraft, heavily laden with fuel, jerked violently. My breath jammed in my throat and the bitter taste of horror invaded my mouth. I was going to die.

Pandemonium was everywhere: brittle sounds of the cabin breaking apart, panels popping from the ceiling at crazy angles. I cringed at the sight of loose luggage flying through the air and bouncing off panicked passengers. A darkened movie screen shattered in a heap.

A flight attendant screamed, "Tighten your seat belts! Tighten your seat belts!" Then another attendant yelled, "Head between your knees ... grab your ankles! Head between your knees ... grab your ankles!"

Before I ducked my head, I glanced fearfully out the window. We were racing down the runway toward the rental car lot, which was crammed with cars. My heart pounded in my chest. An eerie silence blanketed the cabin as I witnessed the fear of death frozen on the faces around me. I dropped my head, gripped my ankles, and immersed myself in a strange union of dread and anticipation.

I had heard that your life replays in your mind when you are at death's door. My life was such a mess; I really didn't want to see it again. Visions of a childhood afflicted by family alcoholism and violence flashed before me. I'd been hospitalized at six years old for malnutrition. My dream of becoming an Olympic skier was scrapped when I needed a heart catheterization at sixteen. My ongoing battle with my weight entailed abusing my body with diet pills and bulimia—repeatedly vomiting, and binging and fasting. I had no real career as an actress—only a series of rejections and bills to pay. Men's faces passed before me; I had loved them, and they spurned me. Unworthy, and on the brink of suicide, now my wish would come true. In a matter of seconds I would die.

The plane was hurtling off the end of the runway with a load of passengers and a belly filled with explosive fuel. Then the unimaginable happened, and an all-encompassing calm descended upon me. Overcome by a rush of warmth and euphoria, I succumbed to a sensation of profound tranquility. The serene calm blanketed me with a feeling of protection. At no time in my life had I felt such love. I wondered, was this what it was like to die? Was this the mysterious culminating grace, or a normal reaction before death streamed down darkness? Did my fellow passengers feel insulated from their fate by this sense of peace and unconditional love? Did they also hear what I perceived to be an inner voice speaking to me?

You were given this life!
What have you done with it?
You can choose to die or
you can make a difference!

As the plane skidded and bounced, I was forced to question my existence on earth. I heard the screech of metal tearing along the left side of the aircraft. Crashing sounds intensified to a deafening clatter. Seconds before slamming into the rental car lot, the plane skidded and ground to a halt. My neck snapped back and my hands flew from my ankles. The aircraft burst into flames and I was entombed in the burning wreck.

The voice ... the voice ...

Have you spent your life
complaining or creating?

The left side of the cabin was already engulfed in flames. The right fuselage was slanted upward, as if someone had jacked it up twenty feet in the air. Flames billowed outside my window. What remained of the left wing was swallowed up in smoke, yet I sat suspended in a state of bliss. A shield of energy encompassed me.

A flight attendant shouted, "Come to the rear! Come to the rear!"

Frightened passengers swarmed into the aisle to save themselves. Robotically, I unbuckled my seat belt and shuffled into the crowd, colliding against bodies whose only care was to escape before the plane exploded and sealed them inside. When I reached the end of the sixth row I spied the exit door, but before I could access it, the pushing from behind popped me out of line like a gumball from a vending machine. I tumbled headfirst onto the tilted cabin floor and slid helplessly on my stomach toward the gaping exit door and the raging blaze outside.

Heat seared my skin, smoke assaulted my lungs, and savage flames engulfed the entire rear exit of the cabin. If this was hell, I wanted out. *Fool*, I anguished, *it's too late for you. Prepare yourself for an agonizing death.* Suddenly, when there was nothing more than air to prevent me from falling, I stopped sliding. I stared mesmerized at the wall of flames. Again, I heard the calming inner voice.

> ***Do you love yourself?***
> ***Do you have a good relationship***
> ***with your family and friends?***

The words resonated in my head as I lay sprawled on my stomach, hands stretched out before me, transfixed by the toxic bonfire. Sweat streaming down my face, I screamed, "No ... no ..." Inches from my body, a flare of red-orange flames seared my skin and left me gasping. When I was only seconds from death, it came: an urgency to fight for life. I needed more time to love and redeem myself.

Time to make things right. I yelled, "I want to live!"

> ***Are you living your goals and dreams?***
> ***If you die today, have you left this***
> ***planet a better place for being here?***

"No ... no ... I want to live!"

Thick smoke and scorching heat squalled inside the pitch-dark cabin. Palpable fear seized me as I stared at the flames. If I wanted to live, I had to walk through fire. I choked back a surge of nausea and struggled to my feet. Step by agonizing step, I navigated through the smoke up the slanted floor until I found myself at the bathroom door. I leaned against it to catch my breath; sizzling hot metal blistered my skin. Hordes of people were converging on the exit door ahead. Flight attendants were valiantly trying to maintain order as, one by one, people vanished through the opening to ... to what? I aimed toward the crowded exit door clogged with people. How would I get out? The answer flashed through my mind.

> **Ask and it will be given,**
> **seek and you will find,**
> **knock and the door**
> **will be opened unto you.**

"Please," I begged an invisible savior. "I don't want to die now. Please let me out." Heart banging against my chest, through a haze of pain I stared in disbelief at a narrow opening on one side of the door, and saw just enough space for someone to slide through. I squirmed sideways through the gap, shrieking as the boiling metal scorched my stomach. A mass of frightened people crowded in from behind, and I screamed at them to stop when my right sandal stuck on a hunk of protruding metal. I twisted and turned, trying to free my foot as I was thrust toward the ramp by a surge of desperate passengers. My leg collapsed into an impossible position and I feared it would be torn from my body. Tears of pain and frustration stung my eyes. To come so far and find death licking her lips once again was unbearable.

"Please," I wailed, "help me." Miraculously, my sandal ripped free and I was catapulted through the opening and onto the slide. I dove downward in a desperate contorted dance, slamming into the ground just as a woman with jet-black hair crawled away on her hands and knees. She cried out for help, then disappeared, engulfed in smoke. My left ankle exploded with pain and my leg crumpled beneath me as I crashed into the tarmac. A hundred daggers stabbed my spine. Pushing the pain from my mind, I appraised the burgeoning flames encompassing the area. After all I had been through, I was still going to burn to death. Why hadn't I chosen a spiritual path? At least I would be prepared for this moment. My protective energy had vanished as quickly as it had appeared. I was going to die.

Rivulets of fuel and flames sparkled in a death dance on the tarmac. Loose asphalt dug into my palms, and viscous fuel soaked my jeans. Thick black smoke rolled menacingly toward me, while volcanic flames shot up from the fuselage, warning of my impending spontaneous combustion. I had come so far, only to face obliteration again. I put my full weight on my right leg and heaved myself to my feet. Excruciating pain erupted at my lower back. I clamped my hands behind me to support my spine and, dragging my left foot, hobbled clear of the flames. When I turned to assess the blazing scene, I was unable to comprehend the picture before me. Was this really happening? Was this my recurring nightmare, and would I soon wake up? Had I known this would happen, and attracted this fate with the power of my negative thinking?

A booming explosion brought my attention back to the present. The evacuation slide I had escaped upon, my wonderful life raft, was now a limp appendage licked by flames. I knew this was no dream; this was real. As real as knowing I'd been the last person to escape from the rear section. I was still alive. Remaining passengers stood helplessly in the doorway, wreathed in fire and smoke. Scanning for alternative escape routes, I gaped in horrified silence as the slides at every exit deflated and burned into putrid puddles.

An elderly couple stood at the next exit door hugging each other while contemplating the twenty-foot drop to the tarmac below. He gripped her arm as they turned and gazed deeply at one another. It was as if I had entered their emotional lives as I perceived their exchange of love. They leapt from their perilous perch as one entity, and vanished into the voracious flames. My eyes searched in vain for a sign that they had survived, while my hands reached out futilely to help them, as I chanted, "Let them live, let them live."

An eternity later, I gasped as I saw the man wobble to his feet and pull his wife from the blaze. Her leg aflame, his face scorched, he doggedly dragged her to safety. I whispered, "Thank you."

Exhaustion bled through bone and into the very marrow of my being. Shaking violently, tears blurring my vision, I clamped my hand over my mouth to hold back my screams and quell my nausea. The bedlam raged on. Fleets of fire trucks roared to the scene, luring more people to leap from the inferno in a final effort to avoid incineration. As people plunged to the tarmac, they were pounded by a pressurized blast of foam from the firefighters' hoses.

A shrill scream tore me from my trance. A woman had fallen and was writhing on the tarmac. I limped over to her and had bent down to help when two paramedics arrived in an ambulance and warned me away. Suddenly, a thundering explosion erupted from the middle section of the multi-million-dollar giant where its fuel tanks lay. The ground shuddered like a massive earthquake, flames shot up like rockets, and black smoke mushroomed up.

A human torch jumped from the rear exit and rolled to the ground. He blazed, screaming, in a frenzy of pain. When a dousing with a fire-retardant foam proved futile, a fireman grabbed him and began flailing at the flames with his heavy gloves. He then rolled the burning man along the ground until the flames subsided. The fellow's head slumped down, his arms sprawled aside his smoldering body, and I knew he teetered on the brink of death, while the fireman did what he could to offer comfort. Witnessing the fireman work so unselfishly to save an injured stranger, I felt a rush of love for both of them and wished I could understand why people so often must experience tragedy in order to express love.

Fifty feet from the broiling wreckage, stricken survivors clustered together and clung to a chain-link fence, their faces jelled into expressions of horror. The passengers pushed their backs against the fence, trying to escape the expanding flames, choking smoke and unbearable heat. The dream ... the same fence as in the dream. This was the same scene I had pictured in my nightmare. I was living my nightmare. Oh no, how could this be? My dream is my reality. The images would be forever ingrained in my soul. I stood alone, sickened by the stench of jet fuel, burned rubber, and flesh. Gagging, I grabbed my throat and massaged my neck to prevent myself from heaving. I kept repeating, "I am alive!" Nearby, a woman clutched her blistered legs, sobbing in pain. The seriously injured lay on blankets, awaiting treatment from medical crews still rushing onto the scene in howling ambulances. I pondered why, in the midst of all this horror, did images of my destiny keep appearing in my mind? What did they mean? As the fire raged on, I heard the spellbinding voice once again.

Your assignment is to help people help themselves.
You will speak and write.
I kept thinking it couldn't be me who would do this. "I can't. . ."
You will have a daughter
late in life who will be a leader.

Standing there in shock, I felt what strength remained draining from my legs. I glanced over my shoulder expecting to see who owned the clear, strong voice, but no one was there. I checked to see if anyone was staring at me, but no one was. I played the message over in my mind. Why did it come to me now, of all times? My resistance to change had been so strong, but now my walls were ripped away. Where did it come from and who sent it? I lifted my eyes to the sky.

It was still early morning in Los Angeles, but the smoke, ominous clouds, and rain had darkened the sky to the color of sludge. A two-car tram from the airline pulled up to transport the ambulatory survivors. Chilled to the bone, rancid, and streaked with char, we were wrapped in blankets and helped into the tram. The windows were steamed and the interior immediately filled with the stench of fuel and fumes from our soaked clothing. Gasping for air, we pounded on the windows until the driver hit the lever to open the doors. We gulped in the smoggy air as though it were pure oxygen.

Exhausted, we finally arrived at the Continental administration building. A temporary triage center was being set up to provide medical treatment and fresh clothing. I limped into the building dazed and aching, urgently wanting to call someone. Someone who loved me. Someone who would care about what had happened to me. Someone whose words of reassurance would soothe my uncertainties and frayed nerves. I needed to make sense of what had happened. Why? Why did this happen? Why was I on this flight? My mind was so disconnected I wasn't sure of anything. This wasn't a dream! This was real! Or could I have died? Was I just imagining that I was still alive?

One of the crew directed me to a conference room where I could use a phone. I got through to my mother, who cried hysterically as I told her what had happened. The previous night, we'd had a major fight about me finding a worthwhile career and making money and she'd hung up on me. Now, all she could think about was that I could have perished and she'd never have had the chance to talk to me again. I spent the entire time reassuring my mom, telling her I loved her again and again. She promised she would call my stepdad at work and tell him what had happened. I reassured her I was okay and would phone her again the following morning. If she needed me I would be home later and she could call. I was so glad I had talked to my mom, but still nothing made sense. I yearned to have someone listen to me and help me figure out the horrific ordeal I had survived.

Next, I called my brother Doug, who seemed disinterested, said he was working and to call him later. I hung up the phone and stared at it. Didn't he understand I needed him now? Knowing him, he probably thought I was being dramatic and making the accident bigger than it was. He disliked that I was living in Los Angeles and attempting to be an actress. He believed I should get a real job. Sitting there in a stupor, I realized my brother was not going to help me make sense of what I had encountered.

Next I called my father, who asked a lot of questions and seemed happy that I was safe, but never said, "I love you." I was hoping that for once, he could unbury his feelings and show some emotion.

After hanging up the phone, I folded my hands on the table and stared at the wall. Where was the comfort I so desperately needed? Who would help me understand why I hadn't burned to death? I couldn't call Mary Margaret because she was on an acting audition. My mind still accelerating; yes, I had wanted to die yet I hadn't died. I gasped and then calmly I said his name, "George." Of course, George. I would call the one person who was always there for me.

George was an unusual man who had entered my life in an uncommon way, almost as if he had been sent to me. Eight years earlier, having been crowned Miss Hawaii, I was walking off the stage when a heavyset gentleman with an Oklahoma accent congratulated me and told me I deserved to win. Something about him was so warm and familiar that I was drawn to him instantly. Some people have a talent for music, others have a knack for investing, but George's gift was a greater understanding of human behavior as it relates to our mindset and spiritual nature. When he eventually predicted certain events, I feared he was weird, but as they came to pass, we became fast friends.

I dialed his number in Oklahoma, and was relieved when he answered on the first ring.

"George, I'm so glad you're home," I blurted out. "I need to talk to you in the worst way."

"Hey, Partner," he greeted me with his favorite nickname. "What's going on? You don't sound yourself."

"It's me all right." *Just not the same me*, I thought, glancing at a mirror on the wall. Red curls lay matted against my scalp, but my smooth, light-skinned face remained remarkably composed and somewhat subdued. My blue-green eyes were rimmed by dark circles, but a new clarity seemed to have surfaced in them. I continued, "My body is bruised and banged up a bit, George, but my brain has experienced an epiphany. Those dreams ... those dreams I told you about, where I was limping away from a burning airplane ..."

"Donna, are you okay?"

"The dream came true this morning. Not a dream but the real thing, like the dream. I don't understand. I nearly died. The nightmares had become so persistent, I tried to reschedule my flight to Honolulu four different times and guess what? I wound up on the original flight this morning anyway. It crashed, and exploded on takeoff."

Dreadful images replayed in my mind, causing my head to pound as I recounted, "It was horrible—people injured, jumping, burning ... the faces ... the fence. In a few fearful moments, life changed for every person on that plane. How does that happen?"

Choked by emotion, I waited quietly. I closed my eyes and envisioned him here in the room with me; a calm forty-something, teddy bear of a man with a kind face and wispy hair. Behind horn-rimmed glasses, his clear eyes revealed compassion and strength of character. I heard the familiar tap-tapping of his pipe in the background. After a long sigh, he said, "Donna, are you sure you're okay? You should be seen by a doctor after such a trauma."

"I'm fine, George, I'm alive. I'm one of the lucky ones, and I already told my family that I am okay. I need your wisdom to help me understand what really happened here. Remember when I moved to Los Angeles to study to be an actress, and no matter how hard I tried, I was rejected and succumbed to depression? You coached me to hang in there and not attempt suicide. You averred that my life would change in five years. George, this is the fifth year. Why do I have the eerie feeling that you came into my life to prepare me for this predestined day?" I chattered on, "I learned today that life is a gift."

"I'm sorry you went through this, but not wholly surprised. It often takes an encounter with ultimate disaster to expand one's awareness of something larger than narrow self-interest. This experience has changed your life forever and will lead you toward greater wisdom."

"I don't understand. I mean I don't ..."

"Donna, you're finally getting the big picture, albeit the hard way. A while back I said you first had to learn patience and vision to know your destiny. Today you earned the right to discover what the future holds for you."

Was that what the calming voice was telling me? The messages were about my future? I waited a few seconds while George puffed on his pipe.

"Today was about transformation. Your real work is to help other people believe they can have a better life. Through your own experience, you can rekindle their hope."

"George!" I was shocked he knew. "That's what I learned today—I mean, it's what flashed through my mind during the plane accident, that I have to help people."

He sighed into the phone. "You know, there's all kinds of people out there who lack confidence, those who choose to exist in the pain they inflict on themselves and others. There are people who are afraid to live because they're afraid to fail, so they don't try anything new. Misery and fear surround those who choose to suffer. Fear is real; you must face it and overcome it. Focus, discipline, and, yes, doing some things you don't like to do, open your world to fresh possibilities. What came to you today was the knowledge that you have the potential to help people."

I didn't have the slightest idea where to begin. "I'm not so sure.

Something came to me today, but I don't think I'm capable of helping other people transform their lives. I don't believe I'm worthy enough."

"Every soul is worthy."

I couldn't believe that George had me chatting away when only an hour before I had nearly died. Strange as it seemed, it didn't stop me from talking. "My life is a wreck. How can I help anybody when I can't help myself?" I continued. "Growing up in a family overrun with addictions didn't give me the life skills to help people. I didn't exactly graduate at the top of my high school class. In fact, I barely made it into college. It was sheer luck that the University of Montana accepted me, and then that Hawaii had just become a state so there was plenty of room at the University. You know I've been struggling for seven years to become an actress. I'm not complaining, but I'm not confident how I'm going to help people."

I waited for his answer, tapping my fingers on the desk. I hated it when he got quiet. "George, are you smoking your pipe again?"

"Doing a little more thinking. Let me ask you: how does a baby learn to walk?"

"Takes one step, falls down, gets back up, takes another step, falls down ... what's your point?"

"I'm suggesting you start work on a life better suited to your talents. You've taken a few steps and fallen a few times, and now you're ready to begin one of the greatest learning periods in your life."

The line was silent, and then he continued, "Consider this, Donna: how did you get out of that plane? Don't answer. I'll tell you. You experienced the gift of love. Like a baby taking its first steps, you walked through those flames."

I smiled with awe. "When I was about to die, I encountered something beyond earthly love, even beyond mortal love. It was a feeling of glorious happiness that kept intensifying. I'd call it ...

supreme love. Do you understand what I mean?"

In a soft, understanding tone George said, "Let's say I've got a pretty good handle on it."

Then a knock came at the door, and an airline employee informed me that a doctor was waiting to examine me at the medical triage.

"Hey, I've got to go and get checked by a doctor. Please tell me I'll see you soon. Are you coming to Los Angeles on business?"

"Let me look at my calendar and I'll call you in a couple of days. Take care and be good to yourself. I'm proud of you, Partner."

My throat burned, my injuries throbbed, and I wanted to go home. I limped down the hall to the makeshift medical clinic and was shocked at the chaotic scene. People were shouting directions and calling for help. Dozens of passengers covered in bandages and attached to IVs lay on stretchers on the floor. It was a scene right out of a disaster movie. Medical personnel and airline employees were frantically running back and forth, grabbing supplies and assisting the injured. A nurse helped me to a chair and then began questioning me. The skin on my arms and legs stung like a severe sunburn. My entire body ached. There were shooting pains in my lower back, and my ankle throbbed. She told me to rest, and that a doctor would see me as soon as possible. As I sat there I learned that the most severely injured had already been evacuated to local hospitals. The rest of us were being assessed here; some would be transferred to hospitals, and others would be released to go home.

Eventually, a doctor ordered a med tech to treat my minor burns and bandage my sprained ankle. After resting awhile, drinking water, and being deemed stable, I was released. A Continental employee walked me outside the terminal to the taxi stand, helped me into the cab, and gave the driver a voucher. I wrapped myself in the airline blanket and mumbled my Westwood address to the driver.

He turned his head and did a double take. "You okay, lady?"

"Yes," I replied in a listless tone, much like I was discussing the weather. "I've just been in a plane accident."

He said, "Lady, you were in the big crash?"

I softly mumbled, "Yes."

Though my body was singed, bruised, and aching, I felt more alive than I had in years. I immersed myself in a spectrum of color, texture, and sound, and in the skyscrapers and stately buildings I had passed so often without noticing. The world was beautiful. I was alive! I gazed at the back of the driver's bald head and smiled. This stranger who protectively wove his cab through traffic wasn't just a stranger driving a beat-up taxi, but a fellow human being who had hopes and fears like me. I sensed the healing process had already begun, though I still had a long way to go. I'd always had a gnawing, unsettled feeling in my stomach that kept me on edge. That quiet desperation and sense of abandonment I had wrestled with for so long evaporated in the plane crash. George was correct. I was spared for a reason. Grateful for today's realignment of my spiritual path, I couldn't help but wonder what lay ahead.

As the cab driver departed, I limped up the steps to my apartment. Only when I was safely locked inside would I let myself collapse from sheer exhaustion. My first thought was to lie down on the sofa, but then I had an overwhelming desire to fall to my knees and pray. I didn't begin my prayer the usual way, where one gives thanks— though I was thankful—nor did I ask for anything. That's why this moment was so unforgettable. I closed my eyes and shared my most intimate thoughts with God.

I know you're listening, God. Though we haven't talked a lot, I know you've always been there when I needed you. In the past, I always asked for this and that. Now, I just want to say how much it means to know you love me and believe in me, even though I had all but abandoned you. I realize now, there is a higher purpose to my life and I want to help do your work. What am I supposed to do? Where do I begin? Please, will you guide me?

I kept my eyes closed, my head bowed, and waited for a sign or an answer. During this time, I sensed I was not alone. I don't know how long I remained detached from my surroundings, reflecting in a reverent state. The answer I sought was eventually revealed to me in a fragmented dreamlike state; a stage, a book, and an infant. After that, I remembered nothing and fell into a deep sleep.

When I awoke, I was lying on the floor curled into a fetal position. Rolling to my knees, shuddering with pain, I struggled to my feet and stumbled into my bedroom on unsteady legs. As I collapsed onto the sheets, my tremors shook the bed. I pulled the covers up to my neck and held them tight around me. I had battled death head-on, but I was safe now, safe in my own bed.

As I drifted toward sleep, I quickly sat upright with the sudden realization that I must not forget what had happened today. I had to chronicle the events and messages, the emotions and the lessons. After removing a pad and pen from the nightstand drawer, my pen seemed to surpass my thoughts, spiraling down the page at its own rapid pace.

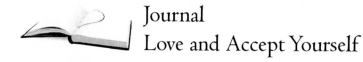 Journal
Love and Accept Yourself

Before the plane crash, I was unhappy and had a death wish. I had no acting career, no love in my life, and struggled to pay my rent and buy food. The words I had screamed this morning—"Let my life change. Let it never be the same. Or let me die."—WOW, those words were extremely powerful. Watch out what you ask for. The four questions I heard during the accident altered my thinking:

Do you love yourself?
Do you have a good relationship with family and friends?
Are you living your goals and dreams?
If you die today, have you left this planet a better place for being here?

How sad that I had answered "no" to all four questions. I want to answer "yes" to these questions. Life can take years to change, or it can transform in seconds. I was shortsighted because I didn't understand what George had been telling me from the day we met.

When you are sick and tired
of being sick and tired
you'll change

I am sick and tired of being sick and tired. For weeks I had been thinking about suicide. From childhood on, I have searched for the reason behind the gnawing hunger inside of me. Now, I understand I did not feel loved.

I believed returning to Hawaii was my only hope. It is a magical paradise for me, a Shangri-la to heal the soul. I thought if I could go back, I could find love or it could find me. Instead, I awakened to real love when I chose life over death in the fiery horror of the plane crash, and discovered there was a higher power who loved me. By confronting death, I understood the importance of life.

Yet, I still have doubts. Today, I love myself, but will I still love myself when I mess up? I should have structured my life differently and not waited around for Prince Charming to appear. Was I living an illusion of becoming a famous actress? Am I sabotaging my own success by not believing I am worthy? People don't need to survive a plane crash to learn about life. Though, I realize now the plane crash was inevitable for me because I refused to change.

From now on, before bed, I promise myself to do two things: first, I will focus on keeping my life moving forward, personally and professionally. I will ask for inspiration and guidance every night. God, help me understand the wisdom that was given to me today.

Today, I claim the lessons I have learned. They're mine forever. Next, at the end of each day, I'll give thanks. I took my life and health for granted with no gratitude, only yearning for more until I almost lost it all. I am thankful to have lived through today, March 1. Oh no—my hand shakes as I write this. What is happening? A fleeting thought flashed by, as if this date had yet to play a greater part in my destiny.

There is a purpose
for everything that happens
Develop your insides
and your outsides will follow

Chapter Two

Focus On Values

Challenges are the mountains you climb in life
What makes the difference is how you handle them
Desperation and inspiration bring change

Orange ... red ... yellow flames surrounded me. Black smoke billowed as I gasped for air. *Suffocate ... I'll suffocate, I can't breathe. Flames, fire ... I'm going to burn to death.*

I bolted upright in bed, awakened by the sound of my own deafening screams. My heart pounded. I gripped my chest as if to keep my heart inside my body. Sweat drenched my nightgown. For several seconds I didn't know if I was dead, alive, or dreaming. I felt around with my hands. I was in a bed, but it wasn't my bed. Every nerve in my body was electrified. I wanted to forget, but the nightmares wouldn't let me. My mind seemed determined to be elsewhere—back inside the horror of the burning wreck. Back with the other victims. Sleep eluded me.

I was in Hawaii. I was physically back in Hawaii, under contract to emcee the Miss Hawaii pageant. I had boarded another aircraft three days after the accident. It was terrifying for me to walk down the jetway and take my seat. When the pilot announced we were cleared for takeoff, my body recoiled. As the jetliner barreled down the runway, a passenger exclaimed, "Look at that!" The words caused me to glance out the window, where I saw it. The carcass of the Continental DC-10 heaped on the side of the tarmac. Starting with a whimper, then gaining momentum, my sobs had erupted.

Tossing back the covers and walking barefoot outside to the lanai, I sat down on a patio chair. The soothing sound of frothy whitecaps washing over the sand calmed my frazzled nerves, and I lounged, listening to the rhythm of the sea until dawn.

At about eight I headed to the beach in shorts and a t-shirt to wade in the salt water and soothe my swollen ankle. I needed time to process the surreal sensations of my life since the crash. When someone spoke to me I felt removed; it seemed like I was two sentences behind what they were saying. Maybe this was a symptom of post-traumatic stress. I stared at the ocean searching for answers. My thought pattern was so jumbled that I couldn't think clearly.

I returned to my room with plenty of time to primp for the pageant. Against the backdrop of a vermillion sun dipping into the horizon, I stared at my long white evening gown. In a few minutes I would need to dress, but I was still processing chaotic thoughts. Looking in the mirror as if to convince myself, I ordered, "Get it together. You're going to be on stage emceeing the pageant. Don't blow it. This is something you've wanted to do for years."

Strange. Why this year? That's what put me on that fateful flight. Did I have to win the pageant years back to be on that exact flight? Was it destiny? A glance at the clock showed time was running out. With haste, I applied body makeup on my arms and throat to cover the red blotches from the burns.

The main ballroom at the Hilton Hawaiian Village was magnificently decorated with a multitude of brilliant orange birds of paradise and torch ginger flowers. There was a buzz of people being seated with the anticipation of seeing who would be crowned the new Miss Hawaii. In the first competitions the girls were judged in their one-piece swimsuits. Next, the contestants graced the stage in their colorful, flowing gowns. The audience held their collective breath as the five finalists were called forward. Now the determining factor would be how each answered her final question. When I'd run for the title, my answer to the question was what had placed me in the lead over the competition.

A judge handed me the fateful envelope as I turned from the microphone and saw the hope reflected on the faces of the contenders. I ripped open the envelope, and began to read off the names. Before announcing the newest successor, my thoughts flashed back to eight years earlier when I took the joyful winner's walk down the ramp. So much had happened since then. I had struggled in Hollywood to become an actress—almost ruining my health with bouts of bulimia— waiting for someone to give me a lucky break, not understanding I had to create my own luck. But that was the past; today was a new beginning.

After the crowning of Miss Hawaii, I walked off the stage amidst tears of joy and defeat. Nearing the exit door leading backstage, I noticed my former agent, Marge.

"Good I found you, Donna," she said. "I heard you would be here to emcee this pageant. I've got a tip on an audition for you tomorrow." She explained that Kodak would be filming a national TV commercial. "Are you available?"

"Sure. I mean yes. I can be there. A national spot, that sounds great!"

Marge and I hadn't communicated in the last year, so I was thrilled she was contacting me for a commercial. As she rattled off more details, I noticed a well-dressed woman standing near the dressing room door.

She caught my eye and smiled. "My daughter was in the pageant. She was so excited and kept insisting it was the best experience ever."

"I am glad to hear that," I said.

"All she could talk about was you, and how you had unsuccessfully tried four times to win, and then finally won on the fifth attempt. That really inspired her."

I remembered telling the story to the contestants during dress rehearsal. After every loss, I swore I would never run again; never, ever, ever. It was proof to me that I wasn't good enough, so why put myself through it again? Then, every year when application time arrived, I found myself filling out the application form anyway. It wasn't until the fifth time of being in pageants that I changed the way I prepared for the competition. I trained with speech coaches, took modeling classes, worked out at the gym, and practiced with photographers. Plus, every day I said to myself, *I am a winner*. When I truly believed I was a winner, I became one.

Alone in my hotel room later that night, I was afraid to face another barrage of nightmares, and I stayed awake until almost dawn reviewing what I had written in my journal and questioning my actions. Could I actually love and accept myself? Doubt crept in like tule fog and clouded my faith. I was on a roller coaster ride of emotions once again. I buried my face in my hands and sobbed, "Please, God ... help me ... help me."

It took focus to get ready in the morning, but I made it on time. Open casting calls were not my favorite. Sliding back the door to the waiting room, there were fifty other aspiring actresses, each one thinking, "I'm the one who's right for this part." Change our hair color and outfits, and we all fit the description. In the next room I could see about thirty male actors waiting their turn. Spying an open seat, I sat down to wait and wait and wait. Luckily for me, I was the last actress to be auditioned. I had a feeling the director couldn't wait until this was over. A tanned, blond actor played my husband as we exchanged lines back and forth. The director and his assistant bluntly asked me a few questions about my experience.

As they turned their backs and put their heads together, I could hear them whisper, "She won't fit the part," and for the two-hundredth time, I heard the words, "Thank you very much, we'll call you if we're interested."

This was the same old rejection that had stolen my confidence on so many interviews before. This time I would fight back. After all, I had survived a plane crash and I had nothing to lose. Turning to the burly director I said, "I don't think you're planning to call me. I've studied for years. I'm qualified. Why not hire me?"

He looked annoyed and said flatly, "You read well but we need someone about five years older."

Perking up, I asked, "What's the wardrobe?"

The assistant tossed me a look that would freeze water, inhaled deeply, then paged through the script. In a distasteful tone she stated, "The commercial calls for a muumuu and floppy beach hat."

I paused to gather my thoughts and then blurted out, "Put one of those full-size muumuus on me. A big beach hat. Pull my hair back, add some makeup, and I would be five years older. I'd be the perfect fit. Thank you." I smiled and spun around and walked out.

The blond actor caught up with me asking, "Are you always that gutsy?"

Glancing his way I answered, "Not until recently."

I had entered that room looking confident, and then wavered, but finally persevered. Refusing to take the initial rejection as a personal insult, I asked questions, even if the answers were not ones I wanted to hear. The plane crash had changed me. I felt a sense of purpose; win or lose, I would stand up for myself. In the past, I always looked for external gratification, and when I didn't get it I was devastated. In spite of what happened today, I actually felt pretty good. Hey, I was alive!

The next morning while in the shower, I heard the phone ring. Reaching for a towel, I ran and snatched it up.

My agent, Marge, greeted, "Hi, Donna, hope I didn't wake you. I'm heading to the mainland and wanted to reach you before I left."

Tension snaked up my spine as I felt the familiar pang of failure. "No problem, Marge. I don't sleep well these days. Are you ... is this about the Kodak commercial?" I asked with studied casualness.

"Uh-huh, sure is. I don't know what you said to the director, but you got the job! They were adamant that it be you, and only you. Wardrobe fitting is today at four PM. I didn't let you know, but the spokesperson for the commercial is Dick Van Dyke."

"Yahoooo! Oh Marge, I am so sorry I shouted in your ear. I'm excited. I will be there for wardrobe and tomorrow, too. Thank you so much for everything. Have a great trip."

It was a blue-sky day when we shot a perfect commercial with an outstanding crew on Honolulu's North Shore. Van Dyke, a true professional with a great sense of humor, told us stories that made us laugh. The backdrop was white sand with palm trees, and we fraternized with bikini-clad sunbathers and surfers. I even had a one-day TV husband for the commercial; tall, dark, and handsome, he was not the blond that I had auditioned with. The irony was that my outfit, a bright, oversized red muumuu with little ocean waves on it made me look twenty pounds heavier; and here I was ten pounds lighter from the stress of the accident. Oh well, that's life.

Later that night, while sitting on the lanai and listening to the ocean, my thoughts turned to George. His hours of patient listening and teaching were finally beginning to make sense. It was time to call him.

I was excited when he answered. "Hey, George, guess what? I finally made it to Hawaii and I'm sitting on the lanai listening to the water and watching a fabulous tropical sunset. So how are things in Oklahoma?"

He sighed. "Don't get smart. It's cold as marble here." Hearing a match strike in the background, I knew George was firing up his pipe. He inhaled a few puffs and said, "I'm thinking about that delicious volcano drink, the one they bring to you all lit up on fire." He chuckled. "Sure would like one of them. Let's get serious for a moment—how are you doing? Are you feeling okay?"

"My body aches and I'm still haunted by nightmares, but I held it together during the flight over here, barely. Forcing myself to fly again paid off. I emceed the Miss Hawaii pageant, and today I filmed a national commercial with Dick Van Dyke." Building speed, I continued, "You remember how I read for tons of parts and never got them; there was always something wrong with me—too short, wrong hair color, too fat." I rambled off a list of judgments.

"Slow down. Let me ask, were you thinking you would not get the part?"

"Actually, all I could think about was landing the job. I knew I was equal to any of the actresses who were competing for the commercial. After all, I had trained appropriately and survived a plane crash and figured if my maker thought I was good enough to stay on the planet, I wasn't about to be put off by some director."

"Aha. That made the difference," George assured me. "Sounds like you got some spunk and fought for the job. Am I right?"

"Yes, you're right." I explained about my discussion with the director.

"That's great. Those TV people had formed an image of Donna Hartley, and you gave them a whole different way of looking at you. You changed their thinking."

"It makes sense the way you say it, but I'm still not sure I understand. Exactly how did I cause them to change their thinking?"

"Confidence," George said. "You became the person you wanted to be. What happened in the past when you lost acting parts?"

I shuddered thinking about it. "Do I have to?"

"I'll do it for you," George said. "Remember calling me after you drove home at ninety miles an hour on the Hollywood Freeway with your focus on smashing into the concrete median? Why? Because you judged yourself by what other people thought of you. How about those times you ate and ate, and then threw up? You had no confidence."

"Like my issues with men, you mean. I seem to repeat that lesson over and over."

"Yup, like the men. You centered your goals and dreams on what they wanted, not on what you wanted, and got hurt."

George had a way of choosing the right moment to show me another path. I heard him at the other end puffing away on his pipe, plotting his approach. I could almost smell the ripe aroma of his cherry tobacco.

Then he said, "When you get the big picture, you make better choices."

"Big picture?" I asked.

"Yup. Attitude does the trick." I heard him draw a few more puffs on his pipe before he said, "It's time for one of my parables, or what you call my Georgeisms."

He began, "Once upon a time in sixteenth-century England, there was a father who wanted to become a merchant, and he had a beautiful sixteen-year-old daughter. Since there were no banks at that time, the father borrowed from a greedy moneylender. He agreed to pay back all the money, with interest, in one year. It was pretty risky, because if he couldn't pay it all back, he'd be locked up in debtors' prison for the rest of his life."

George puffed on his pipe and continued, "The father and daughter worked day and night, but the venture failed. The day before the debt came due, the father went to the moneylender and begged for more time. The moneylender wouldn't budge until he saw the daughter looking as lovely as a budding rose. The moneylender thought for a while and said, 'I've got a proposition for you. I'll marry your daughter to cancel the debt.' The moneylender looked at the father and then at the daughter. Not a word was spoken. The moneylender finally broke the silence and said, 'I'll put a black pebble and a white pebble in my money pouch. If she chooses the black pebble, your daughter must marry me to pay the debt, but you will go free. If she chooses the white pebble, the debt is canceled and both of you will go free.'

"The father and daughter were horrified at the thought of causing the other to suffer the fate of either life in prison or a loveless marriage. With no other choice, they agreed to meet the moneylender in the courtyard at ten o'clock the next morning."

George continued, "Early the next morning the daughter snuck off to the courtyard to plead with the moneylender. When she arrived, she saw the moneylender put two black pebbles in his pouch. She had to think of something quickly or she would be obligated to marry this man she detested."

George chuckled, "When the moneylender held out his pouch to the daughter, she reached inside and clutched a pebble in her fist. Keeping her hand closed, she lowered it to her side near her full skirt and dropped it among the other pebbles in the courtyard. The moneylender yelled at the poor girl for being so clumsy.

"'I'm sorry, it slipped from my hand,' she said. 'Why don't you reach into your pouch and see what color pebble is left?'

"Sure enough, only a black pebble was left in the pouch. The daughter shouted, 'That means I must have chosen the white pebble!' The moneylender had no choice but to cancel the debt and let the father and daughter go free."

George was silent a moment, then continued, "The moral of the story is that no matter how bleak things seem, creative answers are waiting to be discovered if you make up your mind to search for them. That young girl focused on a positive outcome. It's all in your outlook, Donna. Think way back, as far as you can remember, when attitude affected the choices you made."

I sighed. "Okay, all right, just give me a minute. I don't know what difference it makes. Besides, I hated those times."

"What times?"

"When I was younger." I dreaded thinking about it. "In my teens I had so many setbacks—boys, schoolwork, health, you name it. Can't tell you how many times I was dressed to go out and was stood up. After I missed qualifying for the Winter Olympics because of my heart issue, I developed a rotten attitude. To be honest, I had so much conflict in my life, I was always going forward and backward at the same time."

George snickered.

"Though I did have some real hope when I became Miss Hawaii," I continued. "That's when I learned to set my goals and worked hard to achieve them. I was focused and had a good attitude. Things started backsliding when I went to Hollywood. Every ounce of self-doubt I had was revealed during auditions. In fact, I am starting to understand that I sabotaged my career."

I hesitated, beginning to comprehend what George was working up to. "I had an attitude problem, didn't I? I did all the right things— attended acting classes, had updated headshots, and interviewed, but I had no confidence."

"Things weren't so rosy when you first moved to Waikiki, but you figured it out. You loved Hawaii and knew you wanted to stay there, so you found a way. Yep, you sold pots and pans."

"I did make it work in Hawaii. It's even worked again now that I'm back in the islands. What I'm not sure about is how to maintain a positive outlook when I'm back in Los Angeles."

"That's what you have to conquer: fear."

"You can't move ahead by just believing it," I countered.

"Of course you can't. You have to follow up with action, but the first step toward climbing out of a negative pattern is a positive attitude." George paused before he spoke again. "I'm going to ask you to jot down a little list for me. Are you sitting out on the lanai?"

"Yes, it's so gorgeous here, Mr. Wise Man."

He laughed. "Yep, you always have a name for me. All right, don't rub in how wonderful the weather is there. Find yourself a pen and paper and get to work. Write down the five most important things you want in life. I'm not talking about the physical stuff like cars, houses, and diamond engagement rings. I'm thinking love, health, family, security, career, independence, spiritual growth. You know what I mean."

"Today I'm in Hawaii and happy. Why do I need to do this?"

Silence from the other end was my answer. He was holding firm. I finally agreed. "Is there a special way to write this list?"

He chortled. "Let me say this, there isn't a wrong way to make the list. At certain times in your life you might have love at the top; other times you might have health, family, or spiritual growth at the top. No matter—those five values determine how you live your life. Some people take on their parents' values. Others take on the values of people they pal around with. The most important thing is to make your own list. After you write the list, put it in order of importance."

"Okay, I'll do it." I grabbed a notepad, began at the top, and worked my way down as he waited patiently.

After a while, George asked, "Tell me what's on your list."

"Love, health. My back and ankle still hurt a lot from the crash and my skin needs healing. Of course, my spiritual growth, a career, and a family. That's five."

"Good. Now, let me give you another little parable."

"Okay, give me your Georgeisms."

He ignored my comment. "There was a man whom we'll call Pete. Now, Pete had values similar to yours. He loved his wife and kids, kept himself in good physical shape, and had a fine spiritual relationship with his maker. He was a hard worker who loved his job, but still managed to have quality time with his family. Along came a professional opportunity that would make him a lot more money, but the traveling would give him far less time with his family. Pete decided to accept the new assignment, but as time went on, all that traveling and time away from home caused him to resent the job. His relationship with his wife deteriorated and he gained a lot of weight from eating rich foods when he traveled. Today, all Pete has left is his career, which was number four on his value list."

When you live in conflict with your values you're on a collision course with life

"When you get back to Los Angeles, prepare yourself to spend time healing. Get plenty of rest ... that means no late hours."

"I know I want to be a good girl, though it won't be easy." I didn't really want to hear the answer, but I had to ask the question. "What do you think my negative patterns are?"

"I kinda hoped you'd ask that. Partner, you have to keep respecting yourself. Let's wander back a ways. How many times did you run for Miss Hawaii?"

"You know how many times. I was actually a champion at losing."

"I do," he said, "but tell me anyhow because it took you a few years to win. That's a good example of how you conquered what seemed to be a lost opportunity."

I clenched my teeth. "Four pageants, all failed. The fifth time, I won."

"After the fourth, when you thought you'd never win, what made you decide to run again?"

"After I got past the fact that *moi* was a loser, I decided I had to change my mindset. I had to alter my thinking. I kept saying to myself, 'I am Miss Hawaii, I am a winner.' I didn't even tell my family

I was running again or invite my roommates to the pageant. This was it; do or die."

"You changed your attitude to accomplish your goal, which was...?"

"A career. Winning Miss Hawaii would help me become an actress."

Glancing at the clock, I winced when I saw that we had talked for over an hour. I never tired of listening to George. The dear man could make such remarkable sense out of my jumbled life. I knew he was busy with his own consulting business, but he always made time for me. He kept certain areas of his life discreet. He said he was helping other souls who were assigned to him but I never questioned what he meant. Not yet, anyway.

"I adore you, George. You know, whenever we talk about Miss Hawaii, I can't help but recall the day we met. Leaving the stage after receiving my crown, there you were, smoking your bloody pipe and wearing an awful flowered tourist shirt. You didn't look threatening; your face was kind, but it was the scent of your cherry tobacco that brought instant comfort to me. You said, 'Congratulations, you deserved to win this time.'"

"'What? Who are you?' I asked.

"You continued matter-of-factly, 'It's your time. I'm here on Oahu for a couple of days. My name is George and I need to meet you at ten AM at the coffee shop on the corner.' I thought you were weird, but at least not too scary."

George snorted and replied, "Thinking back, it was a bit much to tell you all at once. I'm glad you met with me because I only had a few days to make a connection with you. I used shock value. I kinda figured I had to prove myself by sharing a few harmless incidents to get your attention."

"Even you have to admit that was really way out there. You predicted my car would be towed, my kitchen pipes would burst, and the third step in my apartment would start to creak. The next morning, my sports car was towed away because someone tried to hotwire it, and the wires were everywhere. I went in to wash my hands in the kitchen sink and the pipes burst. I was sopping wet. Going up the stairs to change, I hit the third step ... it creaked ... I froze. I freaked. Wide-eyed and a little scared, I showed up for breakfast."

I waited for George's comment and when he offered none I continued, "I was curious then and I still am. I've often questioned those unpredictable happenings. I'm wondering, are you the wise man in my life who shares your knowledge, the mentor I lean on who gives me insight, or are you really some kind of angel who watches over me? George, exactly who are you?" I whispered into the phone.

After a long pause, George said, "I'll be in Los Angeles in May; we'll talk about it then. It is all about your spiritual growth. There is a lot for you to learn and I promise that when the time is right I will reveal the insights to you. We'll go to that little diner I like. I'll have my coffee, pancakes, and bacon. You'll have your herbal tea and yogurt. I don't understand you health nuts. Maybe you could explain that to me sometime."

It was late when I got off the phone, but I felt keyed up and not at all tired. George had done a first-class job avoiding my question, but that didn't mean I wouldn't ask it again. That was our relationship. I asked him questions, but his greatest gift was that he understood when I would be ready to hear the answers and act upon them. He wouldn't budge if he knew the timing wasn't right.

A full moon glowed with promise and the night was charged with tropical scents and balmy breezes. I went inside, leaving the sliding door open to the sound of the surf. Picking up a pen from the desk, removing my journal from my suitcase, I began to write:

 Journal
Focus on Values

Attitude makes the difference
It determines how far you go

It's wonderful to be back amidst all the splendor of Hawaii, my favorite place in the world. ME! I landed my first major role in a national commercial and called George to tell him all about it. Once again I'm amazed at his knowledge about life, and I learn so much from him. I'm sure my questions drive him crazy, but even if they do, he never stops answering them, except he won't tell me certain things. I wonder who George really is. I pray someday he will reveal the truth so I understand the mystery of why he arrived in my life so strangely.

Today, he helped me discover what my real VALUES are and the need to prioritize and pursue them. My values motivate me. With a little help from my master teacher, I discovered the five things that are important to me: love, health, spiritual growth, career, and a family. That is an impressive list!

Even as I write, I gain greater understanding of what I must learn. First, I must accept myself for who I am. If I'm to get healthy and stay healthy, I need to think about good nutrition and ways to release stress. I am certain I can't go back to the life I had before that had me contemplating suicide. That is correct. It doesn't work for me. Right now I am thankful to be alive one more day. I'M ALIVE! I'm really alive! WOW! My future I can't even comprehend. What's next? What I do know for certain is it will be different, but how?

Chapter Three

Testify or Not

To master conflict
tell the truth

I didn't slow down until I came face-to-face with the refrigerator. I was standing in my girlfriend Mary Margaret's kitchen in the San Fernando Valley.

"Well Donna, it's nice to see you too," Mary Margaret commented as I flew by her. "One of those afternoons? Whatever you find in there, get some for me—I'll put the kettle on for tea."

While attending acting class at CBS Studios, we had become fast friends. I had talked to her on the morning of the plane crash after having another one of those foreboding nightmares. A shiver ran up my spine as I thought of fire ... bodies ... the accident. I gathered up cheese from the fridge and some fresh baked bread, and laid it out on the kitchen counter.

Mary Margaret glanced at the food and said, "Uh-huh. Bread. Cheese. Comfort food. Something on your mind?"

My mind was gushing like a swollen river of muddy water,

reckless and not very clear. "Mary Margaret, I can't do it."

"Do what?"

Digging into my purse and pulling out an official-looking document, I said resentfully, "It's been two and a half months since the crash. I've been subpoenaed by the National Transportation Safety Board to testify, and I can't get out of it either."

I thrust the subpoena in front of Mary Margaret. "Read this. It says here I'm going to be grilled by executives from companies like Continental Airlines, McDonnell Douglas, Goodyear Tire, Goodrich Tire, and Pico Chute Company." I took a deep breath and let it out, then hammered at the subpoena with my finger. "They even listed the Pilots' Association and the Flight Attendants' Association!"

Mary Margaret nodded sympathetically and pointed to a cozy nook bordered by frilly curtains and floral patterned wallpaper. "We should talk about this. Sit down, stuff your face, and have some tea."

I crumpled the subpoena back into my purse and flopped down on a chair. "I can't do it," I wailed. "I've never experienced a situation where my words could seriously impact lives before. I'm scared they'll try to confuse me because millions of dollars' worth of lawsuits are pending. Believe me, I have a crystal-clear recollection of what happened that day. I wrote an absolutely comprehensive report ..."

Mary Margaret looked up from buttering two slices of bread, concern raining down on her lovely face. "Donna, you survived a life-changing plane crash. Now you're complaining."

I sighed. She had guessed right. I was bellyaching.

"If you don't testify, who will?"

"I don't know and I don't care." I sat rigid in my chair avoiding Mary Margaret's piercing gaze.

"Oh, yes you do. You're scared." She picked up the phone and began dialing. "I know exactly who can help you: my friend Phyllis."

A short time later, a stern, athletic-looking woman in a white uniform arrived at the house. Mary Margaret trailed her into the kitchen.

"Hi, Donna," the woman said, holding out her hand to me, "I'm Phyllis, supervising nurse in the burn ward at Brotman Medical Center, where they brought some of the passengers after the plane accident."

When I reached out to shake her hand, pain exploded in my lower spine, and I recoiled. "Pleased to meet you," I said, my hand supporting my back.

"I can see you're in pain and I'm sorry, but I don't believe you realize how fortunate you are. I'm leaving for the hospital right now. Why don't you follow me there?"

I had a paralyzing sense of foreboding, or perhaps apprehension—I couldn't decipher which. I only knew I didn't want to go. My jaws started working in protest, but nothing came out. Mary Margaret handed me my keys and in less time than it took to think up a believable excuse not to go, I found myself following Phyllis's grey compact car to the hospital.

Thirty minutes later we were walking along the corridor to the burn ward. When we reached the entrance, Phyllis paused to pluck two paper gowns from a stack by the door.

"Here," she said, holding out one of the gowns. "Put this on. We have to wear them to protect the patients from infection."

I frowned and did as she asked. Not knowing what to expect, my anxiety level was skyrocketing.

"You'll see patients with disfigurements," she explained matter-of-factly. "Not only have their bodies been damaged, but their spirits as well. We keep them on painkillers and IV drips to replace the loss of fluids, but there is so much physical and emotional pain the drugs can't relieve. Some of the victims were brought here with their skin still burning beneath the blankets."

I couldn't even imagine. "Do you think they'll ever get over this horror?" I asked.

"That's a tough one to answer." Phyllis sighed heavily. "Forget? No. Heal? That all depends on the person. It takes time for people to pass through the psychological stages of what has happened to them. There's denial, anger, grief, self-pity, and finally, acceptance."

I shuddered as I remembered the passenger I'd seen running on the tarmac as a fireman was beating out flames from his smoldering back. Many nights I relived the flashbacks of human torches jumping from the burning plane and rolling on the ground.

"Time for us to go in," Phyllis said abruptly.

I followed her through the doors and into a scene that was far beyond my worst nightmare. I grew dizzy, and bile rose up in my throat at the horrible stench. My legs wobbled, threatening to collapse. I gripped a table to balance myself and ward off the telltale signs of a panic attack. When I was about to cave in, the feeling diminished. Damp with sweat, I accompanied Phyllis from one bed to another, listening to her greet each patient in a casual yet interested way.

They were swollen and deformed human beings, with tubes protruding from their bodies and burn wounds crusted over like rancid hamburger meat. Several times I turned away, repulsed, and then became embarrassed when I saw Phyllis watching me.

A severely burned woman who was propped up in bed moaned from across the room. I recognized her as a fellow passenger. She must have remembered me as well, for she raised a frail hand and waved me over. Frantically looking to Phyllis for help, she nodded, and we walked to the woman's bedside. The elderly woman's voice was raspy and I had to lean in close to hear her.

"You were there," she murmured. "Why did this happen?"

Slowly I shook my head, so choked by emotion I couldn't speak.

"I don't want this to happen to anyone else," she murmured. "No one should have to live in this much pain. Tell me it won't happen again." Then, she turned her eyes toward the wall.

I had to do something. But what? Being in the burn ward was forcing me to look at my life ... to help these people. Suddenly feeling overwhelmed and ashamed of my weakness, I fled the room, tearing my paper gown off as I ran.

When I reached the corridor, I sagged against the wall, gasping for air. I wanted, with every ounce of my healthy flesh, to do something for the dead and injured who couldn't speak for themselves. Afraid, yes, but it was time. Right then and there, with resolve, I made up my mind to testify. If not me, then who?

I felt a hand touch my shoulder and I jumped. I glanced at Phyllis, then lowered my eyes. My actions were unworthy of those suffering people and I could hardly look at her.

"Go on home," she said. "You did well." Like an angel in white, she slipped back through the doors.

I pushed back tears, grateful she didn't criticize me for my wretched behavior. Swallowing back nausea, I ran down the stairs and out to the parking lot, where I fell to my knees and vomited. After I pulled myself together, I stared up at the windows where the ward was located and realized that it could have been me in one of those beds fighting to stay alive.

Slowly, I dragged myself to my feet and walked to my car. When I unlocked the door, the interior of my blue Mustang was stifling. It didn't seem to matter. All I could feel was the pain of the victims. I turned the key in the ignition and leaned my head against the wheel, feeling lightheaded. Now that I had decided to testify, how would I prepare? Within seconds, the answer came to me. George. Of course, I would ask my master teacher for advice.

By the time I reached my apartment and climbed the steps to the second floor, I was exhausted by the sheer weight of my decision. Fear had nestled in my stomach and I was again feeling nauseated. The mere idea of a panel of experts asking intimidating questions was repugnant. Would I be able to do it? What if what I said hindered more than helped? I kept thinking someone else could do a much better job. But I couldn't shake the heartbreaking images of the victims in the burn ward. My mind wouldn't stop its persistent chanting, *If not you, who?*

The phone rang and rang. Where was George? He told me five years ago my life would change, and then when I was twenty-nine he had to talk me out of suicide and insisted that when I turned thirty I would understand. All right, I was thirty and this was the fifth year. I assumed that he meant a great career, a loving husband, and a fabulous house were coming my way. Wrong. Life was changing, but in a way I had never expected.

"Please, Mr. Mentor, pick up the phone. I need you now," I said as the phone continued to ring. I was now personally committed to testifying at the hearing and had less than a week to prepare. *Committed ... committed*, I thought. I had to be committed to my actions before I changed my mind. I picked up the phone and called the lawyers for Continental Airlines and waived my right to sue, so I couldn't be accused of testifying for money. If my testimony was to make an impact, I had to focus on speaking for those who couldn't speak for themselves. I pondered over what kind of advice George might give me. Then, I heard his voice, clear as if he was standing next to me. *Donna, there is a part of you that knows what you should do and a part that's afraid.*

I smiled inwardly. *Yes, George, I understand.* Or did I? Perhaps I could turn to my journal for a plausible explanation.

I sat on the edge of my bed with my journal on my lap. To continue my writing, I felt the need to assess what I had learned up until now. I slowly turned the pages, stopping when certain phrases caught my eye. *Learn to love and accept yourself.* Had I done that? If so, then I was the right person to testify. *Focus on values.* I repeated my values out loud: "Love, health, spiritual growth, career, and family." But where, I asked myself, did the people in the burn ward fit in? The answer came to me immediately. Of course, love, my number one value. My bond with my fellow passengers would give me the strength to testify.

I understood that testifying was not without risk. No matter what those industry-paid experts might say, I would tell my story about what happened on that DC-10. I would relive the crash with every sordid detail. As a survivor, I would explain what safety regulations were missing and which needed to be enforced. I had to be convincing so they would take me seriously. Though I was unable to talk with George, I somehow sensed he was with me in spirit.

During the days preceding the hearing, I spent hours in the library doing research on the causes behind major plane crashes. I called my pilot and flight attendant friends and bombarded them with questions. I was determined to become a worthy spokesperson for the dead and injured. Every night the horror haunted me in my dreams.

Journal
Testify or Not

***Don't look back and wonder
why didn't I try...
do it***

Me? Testify at the inquiry for Continental Flight 603? I don't think so. I can't do it. But I'm subpoenaed; I can't get out of it. Why? Why me? I know most of the other passengers had major injuries and can't speak in court but ... DESTINY ... is the word.

Mary Margaret, a true girlfriend, says it the way it is. Thanks, girlfriend, for being there for me. Love ya.

The burn ward ... what a heart-wrenching experience, but Phyllis was a saint. First, the crash then the burn ward ... DEFINING

MOMENTS. Seconds to change. That is all it takes—seconds. The bodies ... the stench ... the painful images are vivid in my mind. I will. I will fight for my fellow passengers. My voice will speak for them!

I am thankful to be alive. God, grant me the wisdom to speak honestly. Grant me the strength to speak knowledgeably so this never happens again. I'm scared, so stay by my side. Please. Can I ... one person, make a difference?

Chapter Four

For Your Highest Good

The truth will set you free

I trudged down the brightly lit corridor of the Hyatt Hotel next to the Los Angeles International Airport. With each step I kept repeating in rhythm, *I can do it. I'll testify. I'll tell the truth.*

When I opened the ballroom door and saw the hundreds of people already seated in the gallery, my stomach did a flip-flop. I felt overwhelmed. I was reeling from the rush of emotions going through my mind. I never expected this many people. In the front of the room there were seven tables, one for each of the companies being represented. Each table had six representatives with folders in front of them. I surmised each folder was stacked with papers about the accident plus another stack of papers with questions written on them. I noticed that the Air Line Pilots Association and the Association of Flight Attendants were there to represent their personnel. I had to convince myself to put one foot in front of the other and keep walking into the cavernous room. I swallowed hard as I passed the tables and moved to the back to find an empty chair. In fact, it was the last seat in the last row. My heart was racing. I took a deep breath, exhaled, and remembered the victims I'd met in the burn ward. *I can do this.*

The chairman's words boomed impressively from the front of the room. "This hearing is now underway to investigate Continental Flight 603 on March 1, 1978 from Los Angeles International Airport to Honolulu, Hawaii. It is nine o'clock AM on May 30, 1978." He recited the plane's infractions: tire failure, the aircraft's inability to stop after rejected takeoff, and the DC-10's inadequate emergency evacuation system. Then he introduced the technical panel members and delegates seated at the various tables. As the chairman continued I kept convincing myself, *I can do this.*

I listened attentively, reconstructing the event in my mind's eye. I understood how the captain averted an even greater disaster by reacting in 1.7 seconds, well below the normal 4.1 seconds. I silently thanked him. Then I heard, "Miss Donna Hartley. Please step forward to the witness stand." I was the first person called to testify. It couldn't be. *I'm not ready yet.* I began to sweat and my heart pounded so hard against my ribs, I actually believed people in the room could hear it. Inhaling deeply, I rose from my chair and walked as if I were on eggshells up to the witness stand, all the time saying to myself, *I can do this.*

After being sworn in I heard, "Miss Hartley, please tell as precisely as you can what happened to you as a passenger on Continental Flight 603."

Coughing, slowly finding my voice, I started off meekly describing the accident. It was surreal. Suddenly, I was back in the crash, hearing, feeling, and seeing it. My breathing became rapid, my speech pattern accelerated, and I felt like a thousand eyes were on me. When I stopped talking, there was silence. Then I was bombarded by a barrage of questions from the experts.

My knowledge of the technical workings was limited but I had learned enough to express an opinion. Visualizing the passengers who had burned to death before my eyes and the injured people in the hospitals had me ... fired up. I had questions of my own and realized that this was the opportunity, maybe my only opportunity, to speak out. *If not me, who?*

I lifted my head and asked, "Why didn't the evacuation chutes hold?"

From a table in front, a distinguished-looking man with a full head of grey hair replied, "The chute at the rear exit held for approximately 25 to 35 passengers, until the fabric tore away from the aircraft and ignited."

He reinforced what I already knew. The last person to exit from that chute was me. I winced and pushed the memory away. "Some of the passengers came out of the cockpit window. They escaped on a rope. Why don't you have a rope at every door? People had to jump."

Then an idea popped in my head. "I didn't understand the importance of the evacuation instructions. Why not show a safety film because TV gets our attention more than a flight attendant?" I noticed two panel members nodding. They were actually listening to me and taking notes. I was passionate about this never happening again. I wanted to know more about the tires. From what I read, there were three tires that blew; two were retreads, and one was patched.

Different experts weighed in with their opinions. The panel had no clear-cut answers. This would be discussed in detail the next day. Finally, the man who had sworn me in informed me that I could step down. My palms were clammy as I gripped the railing to descend. I had walked willingly into a frightening situation, and now was walking away intact.

I pushed past my insecurities. Walking out of the hearing room, I was encircled by a swarm of media. Dozens of microphones were thrust in my face. One question after another was lobbed at me. My head was spinning. I was sweating and felt like I was going to pass out. When the reporters saw a Continental Airlines executive, their attention was diverted and I broke away and fled outside, gasping for fresh air. Collapsing on a bench beneath a shade tree, I leaned over and held my head in my hands.

I didn't notice a young man sitting down next to me; it was his voice that jarred me.

"Hiya," he said. "I don't mean to intrude on your privacy, but may I ask you a few questions?"

I glanced over at the clean-cut man and recognized him as one of the reporters from outside the hearing room. I didn't feel like talking to anyone, but that didn't seem to stop him.

"What's it really like to look death in the eye?" he asked. "Was it frightening?"

Sensing his sincerity, I felt he was asking more for his own understanding than a storyline. I stared at him for a few moments. He was searching for his own truth so I softly said, "You may think this is strange, but it wasn't scary. When I thought I would die, I felt peace. It's difficult to explain, but in that moment, I felt divine love. I believe a miracle happened. I had what is called a 'white light experience.' I was asked four questions during my ordeal and sadly, the answer to each one of them was 'no.'"

"What kind of questions?" he inquired.

"If I loved myself. Also, if I had a good relationship with my family and friends." Thinking back, I was quiet and then softy said, "Am I living my goals and dreams?"

He nodded.

"If I die today, have I left this planet a better place for being here?"

Looking at the young man I said, "I believe they are the same questions you will be asked someday."

He seemed to be lost in thought. Leaving the reporter to ponder these questions, I headed for the parking lot. Spotting my car, I squinted. I blinked my eyes closed and then opened them. In the distance I could see George leaning against my Mustang, smoking his pipe, and I quickened my pace to almost a jog.

"Hi, Partner," he said. "How is your day going?"

"George," I exclaimed. "What the heck are you doing here of all places? How did you find me?"

"The news about the hearing was in all the papers and on every TV channel. I figured you could use a friend."

"George, you are amazing! You show up at just the right time when I need you. Honest, you won't believe what happened to me. I went to the burn ward and made up my mind to testify. I was so scared that I almost didn't ... well, I am here, and I will come back tomorrow to ..."

"Take a breath, Donna." He pointed his pipe at the car door. "You drive. Let's go to that little fish restaurant in Venice Beach."

"Yeah." I ran to give him a bear hug. "I know the routine, feed you first and then you'll answer my questions."

He chuckled and nodded. "Now you're talking my language, food."

The fish and chips restaurant was a no-frills kind of place that was always busy. Their specialty was fish with French fries and coleslaw, and that summed up your choices. Waiting in line, we talked about the hearing. As always, the Venice boardwalk was swarming with fascinating characters; people gliding by on roller blades, little old ladies in miniskirts with outrageously dyed purple hair, and a tattooed man with a snake around his neck.

George turned to me with a bewildered look on his face, nudged me, and said, "Did you see those people? Don't you think that's pretty strange?"

"What?"

"In Oklahoma, we don't have that kind of stuff going on. You Californians come from the other side of the rainbow."

I laughed. "You are what I would call a conservative man."

The waitress served our fish and chips, and looking at George I said, "I have a pile of questions, Mr. Wise Man."

"Can I eat first?"

I smiled. "Heck, no. I can talk and eat. Can't you?"

George rolled his eyes and cast me an exasperated look. "Donna, what do you suppose I did in a past lifetime to deserve you in this lifetime?"

I noticed the familiar twinkle in his eyes when he said, "I guess there's no getting around that inquisitive itch of yours, so start talking, but first pass me the tartar sauce."

Talking to my master teacher had a soothing effect on my raw nerves. I don't know how he did it, but he could always calm me down. I sure did miss him when he wasn't around. "Say, why has it been so long since your last visit? Where have you been?"

"Meeting with different people. Dallas, Denver, and thereabout," George said between mouthfuls. "Things have a way of going where they're supposed to go. Odd how I got my degree in engineering and here I am doing consulting. I still get the chance to wear my engineer's hat when I meet with inventors to discuss their ideas."

"You're always talking about helping people. I hardly ever hear you say anything about yourself."

He didn't speak for several minutes and I noticed a rare look of sadness had come into his eyes. "I love helping people—it's my calling, but sometimes it's lonely."

"I recall you saying that the spiritual path is lonely because one walks it alone."

"Yup. I said that all right and I'm not complaining, because it's the path to truth. My life shifted when I learned my purpose was to help people. Nowadays, there's so little time and so much work."

George sipped his black coffee and sat back in his chair. "But, it's what I want to do in this life. Donna, do you know how many people on this planet are in pain? I talk to people every day who can't get out of their own way to get on their spiritual path. They don't understand how they're limiting themselves. Why, some people wouldn't know an enlightening experience if it hit them between the eyes."

I nodded. "I can understand that. Take me for example; it took a plane crash to stop the merry-go-round I was on. May I ask you a serious question?"

George threw up his hands and chuckled. "Here we go again. Can I still eat? I need to have enough energy to answer all those worldly questions you have burning inside."

"I want to talk about my testimony. When I got on the stand, I was committed and never wavered from what I wanted to accomplish for the victims." I took a deep breath and exhaled. "I had a solid sense of purpose and everything was clear. Was this a one-time fluke, or can I be like that again? Will I have the ability to make the right decision and follow through?"

George's eyebrow arched up like a caterpillar in motion. "I just lost count of all the questions." He swallowed the last of his fish, and stated, "What you did today was for the highest good."

I tossed him one of my "I don't get it" looks.

"I'll explain by telling you a little story."

I scrunched up my nose while asking, "Another Georgism?"

"That's how we learn. Simple little stories. Anyhow, this happened years back, in Oklahoma City. The cold was so bitter it froze your teeth. I had gone to an appointment downtown and forgot to lock my car. When I returned, I found a wino had crawled into the back seat and fallen sound asleep. A rational mind might think, call the police, get him out of your car and out of your life. But I had a feeling about this guy and my gut told me he was a good man who had gone astray with drink. So I shook him awake, and yes, he was a mess. Took him to a little coffee shop and we drank I don't know how many cups of coffee until he started to sober up. His name was Earl and he told me a sad story of how he lost a successful business, causing his wife and kids to lose respect for him, all because of his drinking."

I leaned back in my chair and listened as George continued.

"I asked him if he really wanted to stop drinking. He hemmed and hawed and said he'd like to stop, but he'd tried and failed several times. He didn't think he could. I'm sure you get the dismal picture. I asked him if he loved his wife and family and if he wanted to get back with them. Earl assured me he did, but said she wouldn't take him back as long as he was drinking. I asked if he wanted to be a success in business again. Earl said he needed to support his family and he liked hard work better than he liked being drunk. I looked him straight in the eye and said, 'If you could stop drinking, get on your feet, make some money, and get your family back, would you be willing to help people?' Earl didn't have the foggiest idea what I was asking, so I rephrased the question, 'If you can stop drinking, do you suppose other people can stop drinking?' Well, he thought about it and decided that if he could do it, anyone could do it. I made him promise that if I helped him get his life back, he would have to help others."

George was entirely into his storytelling mode now. "We met every day and Earl sobered up. I bought him some clothes, got him a job, and I'm not saying it was easy. He had some tough times staying away from drinking. I made it a point to be there when he needed me, and sometimes when he thought he didn't. Nope, it wasn't easy. Earl had to take a hard look at his past and where he was in the present. It was my mission to show him where he could go in the future. Well, in time, Earl got back with his family and eventually wound up owning a huge meat-packing plant."

I almost dropped my fork. "George, that's the Earl I met! When you ran out of your cherry pipe tobacco and I was visiting you I had to drive all the way from Tulsa to Oklahoma City to pick it up. You said you needed it for thinking. Earl had it shipped in for you and I picked it up from him. Such a nice man. Wait a minute. Isn't ... isn't he the guy who worked with young people in Alcoholics Anonymous?"

George nodded and smiled. "He's the one. He kept his promise and helped hundreds of people."

I thought for a moment about the way Earl had conquered his hopelessness. "How did you know when you found this wreck of a man in the back of your car that you could help take him from the depths of despair and show him the light?"

"Donna, it's always up to the individual."

When you get sick and tired of being sick and tired, you'll change, echoed in my mind.

A very attractive couple passed our table, holding hands and laughing. "Look at that. I envy those two people. They seem so in love, so happy. Is that ever going to happen to me?"

George waved his hand at me. "You're judging by what you see on the outside. Do you know if those people are happy? Maybe they've piled up tremendous debt to look good on the outside. How do you know they don't fight all the time? You've got to learn to look beyond the outside."

Staring at George I said, "Okay, okay."

"Now let's talk more about today. During the hearing you had confidence and you acted on the highest good for you and the passengers."

I blurted out, "At first I was so nervous. I thought those bigwig airline people would discredit my testimony because they didn't want to pay out millions of dollars in lawsuits."

"When you're confronted with a major decision, always ask if it's for your highest good."

"George, I ask questions every night, but what does highest good mean?"

"The highest good is what you ask for in order to make the best choice in any given situation. You ask the Universe for the answer that best suits you and every other person or thing involved in the situation. Whatever the outcome, you ask that the highest good be served. You look a little confused," he said.

"I still don't understand what that means," I stated.

"You want it to serve you on all levels. Will it teach you a lesson? Will you grow from the experience?"

"Can you give an example?" I asked as I leaned forward on the table.

When his eyes squinted, I knew he was thinking of another Georgeism. After a bit, he said, "What if you see this car you really like? You say, 'I want that car.' You write out a check and buy it. What you don't know is that the engine is going to blow up in a couple of weeks, and you're going to have to spend a bunch of money to have it replaced. This is what you need to do when you want something. Get real clear. See it in your mind. Say it out loud. Ask if it's for your highest good. Then, trust your intuition. Now this is the part you're not so good at: it takes patience."

"Okay Mr. Miracle Worker, a light bulb is finally flickering on. I'm starting to understand that intuition helps me seek my highest good, but when the answer comes, how do I make it happen?"

He pushed his plate away, empty but for two shriveled-up fries. "You get a higher vibration, what I call the knowing. You focus on three levels: your subconscious, conscious, and higher consciousness."

Trying to make sense of what he said, I thought I understood, but then it slipped away. "Do you mean I should focus on a certain outcome?"

He nodded. "The more focused you are, the higher the vibration, and the more positive energy you have to create what you want. Come on, you're a perfect example of that."

My mouth dropped open. "I am? Me?"

"You focused your energy in Hawaii. What were you doing for a living?"

"I sold pots and pans door-to-door, but you know all that," I said, cocking my head.

"And you put yourself through college, and got a teaching degree. Didn't you buy a sports car and travel to Europe? Didn't your cookware money help you win the title of Miss Hawaii?"

I rolled my eyes and said, "Gee Mr. Wise Guy, to listen to you, it sounds like it was all fun."

"The point is, you put yourself on the path to success. Sure, people and events will come along to try and knock you off your path. From time to time, we all revert back to our old negative patterns. When that happens, you have to focus forward, know your intention ... your goal, and get moving in the right direction again."

"I understand," I said. "But why can't I do this all the time?" No sooner had I asked the question than the answer came. "I think I know the answer to my own question. There was a reason why I was on Flight 603 to Honolulu."

He nodded thoughtfully. "Your dreams told you about the crash, but you wouldn't slow down long enough to understand the message, which was that your life would crash unless you changed. You didn't change, so the plane incident was there to make you stop and open your eyes to a new life. How many nightmares came to you before the accident?"

"A bunch. I even threw up before I left for the airport that morning, and I was the last person to board the plane." I dropped my head for a moment. remembering. "I booked several other flights and then ended up on the original one. When I checked in I demanded that my seat be changed from the left side of the plane to the right. I didn't plan to, but it just came out of my mouth. I was adamant. The question is ... are certain things predestined?"

"You had the opportunity to alter your self-destructive path. You didn't choose to," George paused and sipped his coffee, "you had to be on that plane. It changed your destiny but it was not your time to die. That's why you intuitively knew to change your seat."

"You are destined to have three important lessons, and this was the first."

He said it so nonchalantly I almost missed the importance of his statement. My voice quivered as I asked, "What ... what are you talking about? When?"

He raised his hand and firmly declared, "Not now—the timing's not right for you to know. Tell me about what made you decide to testify."

I was frustrated he wouldn't tell me more. I gathered my thoughts to explain in detail about the hospital visit. Then I slowly said, "My trip to the burn ward convinced me. The experience was heart wrenching, so intense that I actually felt their pain. I never want that to happen to anyone again. It was awful." I fought back the tears.

"It's called compassion," George said gently. "Compassion gave you the courage to tell your story on the witness stand and convince those powerful people they need to do something. Sometimes we need to experience a life-altering event before we can help other people. In your case, it was helping those victims. Everything that happened to you, beginning with the subpoena, going to Mary Margaret's house, meeting the nurse, and visiting the burn ward, was no coincidence."

Pent-up tears streamed down my cheeks.

George sighed. "It's okay to cry." He handed me his handkerchief. "You've been through a lot."

He looked like he was in a trance as he slowly spoke. "Safety regulations will be altered because of your testimony. In the future, you will board an aircraft and watch a short safety movie, thanks to your suggestions at the hearing today. You'll also see other changes."

He reached for his pipe and rose from his chair. "I need a smoke, and some fresh air would do you good."

Exiting the restaurant, I decided I had a full load of lessons for one day. I still wondered if the flashbacks would ever go away. Would I be able to laugh again?

George was heading for the ice cream stand like he was on a mission. "What flavor are you going to have, Donna?"

"I don't know. Not any. I don't feel like it."

George stopped in his tracks. "I don't think I've ever heard you turn down ice cream before. Humph. Well, I'm going to have vanilla, maybe strawberry."

I wiped away my tears and blew my nose. "Boring. Really, really boring. Hmm, maybe I'll have chocolate chip. Are you having one scoop or two?"

George put a match to his pipe and began puffing. He blew out sweet-smelling smoke and said, "I'm getting a Santa belly. One is enough for me."

Sprinting over to catch up with him, I declared, "You'd make a great Santa Claus; I should call you Mr. Claus."

He gave me a look that seemed to say, *Why me?*

"Really, you're the kindest man I know. Speaking of kindness, I'm going to be nice to myself. I've changed my mind and I'm having mocha almond fudge on top of chocolate chip. Hey, why the look?"

George grinned. "Not me, go for the double scoop."

I turned toward the sea and inhaled the cool, salty air. "Look out there, the white sand, the sparkling blue water."

George paused to study the panoramic view of the splendid Pacific, the seagulls dipping into the water against a backdrop of sun-drenched sky. "Yes," he said, "life is very beautiful."

 Journal
For Your Highest Good

Ask if it's for your highest
good, spiritually, mentally,
emotionally, and financially

So much has happened. I have been through more than I care to remember. I can never look at life the same. It's so fragile. How do I start the healing process and put my life back together? I need to clarify what I've learned. Today I discovered a part of me I didn't know I had. COURAGE. George made me feel good about me testifying. He has got patience when it comes to me.

I'm aware that life's journey has ups and downs—that's putting it mildly. I see now the plane accident was a powerful lesson in love. Yes, I must learn to love and accept myself more for who I am, even with my flaws. But I did understand something important about myself. I could do it. I could make a difference. I took that witness stand and spoke up. I had PASSION. I am appreciative that George is a powerful teacher and that he never gives up on me. I ask the Universe to guide me in all things. Lots more to learn. What is next? Next ... what is next?

I will do what is for my highest good

Part II

The Healing

Chapter Five

The Power of Mentors

When the student is ready
the teacher appears

I had always dreamed of helicopter skiing in the Cariboos. I had spent endless hours planning and organizing this trip for a group of skiers so I could ski for free. Despite my injuries, I was determined not to let anything prevent me from realizing my dream. Wanting to celebrate my life while basking in the crystal-clear beauty of acres of untouched now and skiing the white powder, here I was. I had envisioned this since I was a teenager.

The Canadian Cariboo Mountains were even more beautiful than I imagined. I felt enveloped by a sea of silence and a landscape unchanged by evolution. The snow glistened like diamonds and a blazing sun glazed the mountain peaks vanilla-white. As grateful as I was to finally be here, I couldn't help but feel the timing was all wrong. My body was weakened by the accident and I worried I might not be strong enough to handle the challenge of rugged mountain skiing.

There were thirteen in the group, including Cliff, an ex-boyfriend. I thought we could at least be friends during this excursion. A consummate television producer, his idea of success was owning an expensive car, dining at the finest restaurants, and draping a glamorous woman on his arm. The trip had been planned when we were still dating. We were together off and on for almost a year. His work schedule was demanding, but I thought if we got away to Canada and skied for a week ... well, maybe things would be different. Right before the accident we broke up and after the crash I had to move forward. I didn't know what that meant yet; all I knew was I couldn't go back to the painful time of my past.

I flashed back to the last time I'd been with Cliff. We had spent the day at Mammoth Ski Resort and I was starving after a morning of skiing. When we sat down to eat, I commented I could eat one of everything on the menu, but would settle for a burger with the works.

Cliff let his eyes wander to my thighs. "You aren't really going to eat that are you?" he asked disdainfully.

His tone and implied disapproval left me feeling fat and unattractive; so much so, I ordered a small salad and water. It was minutes later when the waiter placed a huge burger, fries, and a chocolate milkshake in front of Cliff. I had to close my mouth and not say anything. During lunch, I saw his eyes spark with interest. The subject of his admiration was a Hollywood-looking brunette wearing a tight designer outfit. In his own insensitive way, I knew Cliff was rejecting me. Throughout our relationship, his career and everything connected with it came first. His negative comments about me and his wanting someone that fit his image cut to my core. I didn't have to guess the relationship was over. The trip back from Mammoth was a strained six-hour car ride in which I struggled to hold on to my composure. My thoughts focused on dying.

Since the ski package was nonrefundable, Cliff was part of the helicopter trip whether I wanted him there or not. Rather than focus on our failed relationship, I was ecstatic to be in the middle of nowhere, between Vancouver and Calgary, about to experience the best powder skiing in the world.

A slim, tall man in his late thirties, wearing a bright red ski suit, introduced himself as Raimund, our guide. His eyes were deep blue, the color of a clear mountain lake, and his tanned, weathered face was framed by tousled blond hair. He pointed to the helicopter and directed us on board. Riding in a helicopter for the first time, I felt lightheaded; not from fear, but more from a ripple of expectancy over what could happen. I eventually mustered up the courage to glance out the window. The scenery was breathtaking. No civilization, just pristine snow-covered peaks, one after another. An unspoiled paradise cloaked in peaceful solitude.

The only negative was the ex-boyfriend, acting as if we were still an item and trying to get back in my good graces. I almost laughed when I saw him express a smile of approval as he looked me up and down. Little did he know that my weight loss was the result of post-plane-crash stress. I guessed he was feeling an ounce of guilt about how he treated me before the plane accident. My nearly dying might have given him some insight as to what was important in life. Well, maybe ...

The helicopter dropped us off at the top of the world, on a flat peak that descended straight down on three sides.

"Pair up!" Raimund ordered in his Austrian accent.

Cliff yelled, "Donna, you're with me."

I weakly waved my hand at Cliff. Our guide handed out little yellow beepers and explained in a clipped accent how to use them in case we were buried in an avalanche. "Never ski alone. Never ski before guide, eh. I set pace for each run. I go first, then signal. You follow."

An accomplished skier, Raimund sliced through the snow like quicksilver. Partway down, he stopped, raised his ski pole high in the air and swung it around, our signal to follow. Dazzling powder flew in all directions as my companions barreled down the mountain with Cliff in the lead, yelling at the top of his lungs. *Wait for me?* No way, it wasn't in his personality. No one was going to hold him back. Alone and a little frightened, I finally pushed off.

The snow was soft as satin, and more beautiful than any other I had ever experienced, but I struggled with every turn. When I reached the group, I wiped out and tumbled down at Raimund's feet. The group laughed at my clumsiness. I felt the heat of embarrassment flood my cheeks and forced down the urge to ski away from everyone.

"It tricky. Don't worry. You do fine, eh," Raimund reassured me. He turned and again skied ahead. When he signaled, I hung to the back of the group and skied fairly well, considering what I had been through. All I ever glimpsed of Cliff was the back of his head. Each downhill run required a helicopter ride back up the mountain. By the third run, I had gained more confidence in my skiing.

Our group met for a brown bag lunch at a scenic clearing atop the majestic mountain. *So this is what is felt like to be on top of the world.* Stunning! The vibrant sun had warmed our bodies by the time we were finished eating. Raimund announced that we were going to ski a full 5,300-foot run he had pegged "the Legburner."

The Austrian guide looked over at me and said, "Donna, you with me."

I was shocked. I sensed he considered me a rather substandard skier and felt embarrassed by how the others had reacted earlier when I fell. "No," I protested, "I really can't do ..."

"Yes, you can," he said, gazing at me with his penetrating blue eyes. "I do half of figure eight, eh. You cross my tracks. You make other half."

My mind kept protesting, *I can't do it, I just can't do it.* Raimund and I were separated from the rest of the group while they prepared to board the helicopter. I shook my head. "I'm sorry, Raimund, but I'm not in shape to follow you down the mountain. Let me stay toward the rear and then if I fall, no one will see me."

"I've been watching. You do it. Live in moment," Raimund said softly in his Austrian accent. "Why be afraid of what others think? You ski well, eh. Relax. Stay one with mountain."

Cliff walked over and insisted, "Donna is skiing with me, Raimund."

The guide shook his head. "No. You never stay with her. She ski with me. I know she is fine. Cliff you go last down mountain."

"You'll make a fool of yourself, Donna," Cliff murmured, low enough for only me to hear.

Cliff didn't know it, but he had done me a favor. I was determined not to run from this challenge and to follow Raimund down the mountain. In the past I had run from what I wanted and had settled for second best so many times, letting myself be ruled by fear. I had beaten my doubts before by becoming Miss Hawaii. This was another opportunity to break my negative pattern. Staying in the background wouldn't build my confidence. I had to believe I was a winner, no matter what.

Raimund adjusted his goggles and gave me a long, meaningful look. I watched him shove off and begin his effortless turns, one after another across the new-fallen snow. It was obvious he was one with the mountain and the outdoors was his natural domain.

I pushed off and began my turns, carving through Raimund's tracks. The heat in my thighs intensified with each turn and my ankle throbbed, but the reward of accomplishment was worth the pain. Crossing his tracks like I was dancing in a snow ballet, I flowed back and forth. Breathless and grinning, I slid to a stop within an inch of Raimund's ski tips. "I did it, Raimund," I shouted. "I did it!" The searing pain in my thighs didn't matter because, like the mountain, the message emerged crystal clear. "I had to go for it."

We clicked our poles together overhead. "Life not so bad, eh? It pretty terrific."

The sun was setting and the crescent moon rising when we made our last run down the mountain. A picture-perfect day; a day etched in my mind forever. I looked up at the sky and said softly, "Thank you. I am blessed to be alive."

Dinner was a delicious feast of roast beef, mashed potatoes, gravy, and homemade pie. Hungry was an understatement. I don't think I'd ever eaten so much at one sitting. We had burned up more calories than I had in the last month.

After dinner, Raimund called me over to his table where he was making the schedule for the next day. As I passed, Cliff gave me a grumpy look that implied something scandalous was going on with our guide and me.

Raimund motioned. "Sit down. Not so goot with him, no?" he said in his broken English.

I shook my head and sighed. "No, not so good with him. Seems I pick men who are emotionally unavailable."

"Why you sell yourself short?"

His words offended me at first. Then I realized Raimund was only demonstrating concern. I shrugged. "I can't remember a time when I didn't feel this way. I've spent my entire life trying to look my best and be the best. I never thought anyone could really care about the person who was plain old me." I sighed heavily. "The plane crash compelled me to change. I can't go back to the person I was—that doesn't work, and I don't know how to go forward to be the person I want to be."

Raimund squeezed my hand. "A plane crash? You in plane crash? When this happen?"

"Yes, I was, but I really don't want to talk about it now."

"Of course, I sorry. I didn't mean pry," he said, and then paused. "You ski with guide Mike tomorrow."

"What about you?" I asked, feeling a little wounded.

"Me ski with slow group, eh. You do fine where you are."

The next day was another glorious and memorable ski time with fresh powder flying in every direction. However, my back injury was aggravated and I tired before the rest of the group. Cliff made it a point to call me a quitter when I decided to return to the lodge with the helicopter refueling team.

A long nap sounded good. Later that afternoon, one of the group woke me and asked if I wanted to go to the guide's house for a sauna. The house was actually a small chalet overlooking a lake, and a short drive from our cabin area.

I lasted only twenty minutes in the 145-degree sauna. When I saw no sign of Raimund, I asked where he was and another guide pointed me in the direction of his room. I walked a few steps down the hall to the second door on the left. Knocking softly and waiting, a sleepy voice answered, "Ya?"

"Raimund, it's Donna."

The door opened and there he stood, barefoot, wearing only his blue jeans. I lowered my eyes, feeling embarrassed.

"Come in," he said and opened the door wider. "What surprise."

His big smile made me feel a little more at ease. I entered saying, "I just finished baking in the sauna and decided to come up and say hi."

"Your cheeks rosy, eh."

It was a flush of sudden shyness, although the sauna did its part too.

He patted the bed, his tone serious. "Come sit. We talk." I sat down on the edge of the bed and waited for him to say something. "I like you, Donna," he said, "I think of you too often. You see, I married."

How could I know he was married? The third finger on his left hand was barren. But, perhaps in other countries, a man's wedding ring wasn't such a big deal. I felt foolish and said, "Oh, Raimund, I didn't know."

He gazed deep into my eyes. "I could be with you. My wife never know. But, is not honest. I would know. I promise she stay in Austria and work. I come to Canada and work. We trust each other. We have much deep love. If I do wrong, I would be dishonest with her and myself. I am not man for you, Donna. He will come someday."

Raimund's blue eyes revealed a warm glow when he spoke of his wife and I understood the tremendous difference between Cliff and Raimund. Cliff communicated in a way that was indifferent and often hurtful. When Raimund spoke, he gave me insight. I smiled and said, "It's okay. I ... I ... but, I'd sure like to know when *he* will happen."

"When time is right, Donna," he said sincerely. "Nature best healer. You doing right. Then heal inside ... your vibration attracts."

"What do you mean by vibration?"

He frowned, rubbing his palms together like he was searching for the right words. "When you on higher consciousness, you attract man on higher consciousness. When happens, you know. Be kind to yourself. Be with nature. Know you have worth."

I glanced at Raimund and sighed. "When you say nature, do you mean God?"

"I mean little of both. They are one." He stood, held out his hand, and smiled. "Now, I take you back to cabin, eh."

During the ride back, Raimund asked questions about the plane crash I had alluded to earlier. While he listened attentively, I filled him in on some of the details. When we reached the cabin, he gave me a tight hug and spoke, "Do not worry. You learning magic of life." He leaned over and kissed my cheek.

I paused at the door of the cabin when I saw the curtain flutter at the window. A light blinked on and Cliff threw open the door.

His face flamed beet-red beneath his recent tan. "You were with him! We have to talk! Now! I'm tired of you making me look like an idiot."

I tossed him a disgusted look.

"You have to be with the best-looking guide, the best skier. You won't be with me, Miss La De Da, but you spent the afternoon making love with *him*. Didn't you? Answer me," Cliff snorted.

His words were raw and angry. I stared at him and calmly said, "I won't waste my breath explaining, because you are incapable of understanding."

A look of surprise crossed his face and he softened his demeanor. "I care about you, Donna. I thought this trip would get us back together."

His whiny tone seemed artificial, almost pathetic. "Too late. You don't care about me. All that matters to you is to be first. When you look at me, all you see is whether I match your idea of the perfect woman."

I didn't want to hold back any longer. I wanted him to know exactly how I felt. "Actually, it doesn't matter what you think anymore. If I got sick or needed you in a crisis, would you be there for me?"

Cliff's blank stare was my answer. I said, "Just as I thought. Cliff, you and I are history." I suddenly felt I had to get away from him.

"Have it your way," he shot back. "I'm going to dinner ... without you." He walked out and slammed the door so hard the pictures on the wall shook.

The morning of our final day was glorious. The fresh lay of snow was fluffy and exquisite. My skis swept down the mountain on wings and I was charged with immense energy. When it came time to leave our enchanted wilderness, I was surprised to see Raimund packed up and ready to join us on the bus.

"I am flying from Vancouver tonight," he said, "returning to Austria."

When the bus arrived, Cliff broke from the group to board behind me. He nudged me to the back of the bus and took the seat next to me. I didn't want to be near him. But when I stood up to move, he blocked my way with his arm.

"You're making a fool of me. You're not sitting with him," Cliff blurted out.

I was furious and didn't care who heard me. Speaking loud enough for the entire bus to hear, I ordered, "Let me out, Cliff. Now!" He dropped his arm down as I slid past.

I hurried to the front of the bus and sat down beside Raimund.

He smiled. "He, as you say, history?"

I chuckled. "You bet." Changing the subject, I continued, "This will most likely be the last time we talk and I wanted to ask you something."

He turned to me with an intense expression saying, "Ask."

"Why is it when I first met you, I instantly felt I knew you? It's hard to explain but I was drawn to you. It seemed so natural and sure enough, I ... I ..."

He nodded, suggesting, "Maybe in past lifetime we know each other."

"What?"

"Perhaps knew each other another time. People get special insight. You felt connection."

I didn't know exactly what he was saying but I knew there was some truth to it because I felt that same connection when I met George.

Raimund turned to me as we were leaving the bus, and with a perceptive look in his brilliant blue eyes averred, "In another lifetime, Donna, meet again."

Journal
The Power of a Mentor

Words and thoughts
are powerful

Just as George predicted, when the time was right the teacher would arrive. Raimund's insight altered my thinking. He is all about living in the moment. When you ski the mountain, don't worry about the past or the future—LIVE in that moment. I didn't really understand that outlook. I used to wind up missing today, hoping that tomorrow would get me what I wanted.

The best healing time for me is the simple lasting joy I get from nature, standing on a mountain top and gazing down at the dazzling white powder, fresh, cold air on my face, and the freedom of skiing. I love it.

This ski trip had some eye-openers about relationships. To say that Cliff and Raimund were totally different is an understatement. My pattern in the past was to choose men who couldn't love me because I really didn't love myself. Now I have more self-respect and I must learn to choose differently.

Universe, I ask to learn to live in the moment. I ask to only be in healthy relationships. Thank you, God for the lessons I learned on top of the Canadian mountains. Those mountains made my soul feel ALIVE!

Believe in yourself and
live in the moment

Chapter Six

One More Mile

*When change happens from the inside
the outside also changes*

Almost six months had passed since the crash. I was a budding actress who had worked with Robin Williams, John Ritter, and Richard Pryor. I believed that being thin and beautiful would insure more success. My body was screaming for help. After years of bulimic behavior and taking diet pills, I strived to be healthy, but was inconsistent in my approach. I would exercise like I was training for a marathon one week while eating nutritious foods, then the next week I'd stuff myself with junk food and lie around my apartment feeling lousy. My energy level was bouncing up and down like a yo-yo and I knew this was not working.

The seeds of bulimia were sown early in life by my family, who admonished me if I gained a few pounds and later, by finicky men I dated in Hollywood and by the once-over I received from casting directors. It was more than once I heard, "When you lose ten pounds, come back and we'll talk to you." I became obsessive about my weight and I knew it was only a matter of time before my eating disorder became life threatening. I solemnly promised myself I would not throw up another meal.

My negative pattern had to change. It was the plane accident that forced me to take a long, hard look at myself. Now was the time for action. I signed up for a month-long endurance program at the Ashram Health Retreat, nestled in the mountains of Calabasas, California. I should have realized this would be an intense program because I was not allowed to bring my own car. A driver was sent to pick me up at my apartment. When he turned down a long, winding dirt road, I gazed at my surroundings and realized it was a very long walk, and I mean miles and miles, to the nearest fast food. I reminded myself again the purpose of this boot camp was to learn how to eat healthy and get physically strong.

After being dropped off at a large, rustic house with my one duffle bag, I entered the front door that led into a spacious main room. Above the fireplace a uniquely carved wooden sign read:

Be still and know I am God
Be still and know I am
Be still and know I
Be still and know
Be still
Be

I was certain my sojourn would be more than a physical experience. Just as the plane crash opened my thinking to spiritual enlightenment, this retreat would offer another challenging path to wisdom.

The main house had five bedrooms, a kitchen, dining room, and a large living room. With eight women enrolled, two of us would share a plain but practical bedroom. We were each given an orange sweat suit and informed we would receive a clean one each morning. I grinned at the irony of the situation. Being a bit vain about wearing certain colors, I noted that this shade of orange, along with my red hair, made me look like a fruit compote.

A tall, solid, blond Swedish woman with a pronounced accent introduced herself as Catharina, the director of the Ashram. Extremely energetic and radiating health, Catharina's brown eyes sparkled.

"Ja, Ja, ladies," she said after appraising our little group, "we are here for fun. Can you believe it?"

A woman who was a return inmate whispered that Catharina was dubbed the "laughing saint." When she disclosed her age, it was hard to believe this together woman was only a year older than I.

The next day began with a 6:00 AM wake-up. Sunlight was just beginning to stream down on the mountains outside my window as I struggled into my orange sweat suit. Heading up a steep incline to the meditation dome, not quite awake, I mumbled to myself, "Remind me why I paid good money to come to this forsaken place?"

Inside the dome, hundreds of crystals swung from the ceiling, bathing us in a spectrum of colored lights. The soft sounds of flute music gave me a sense of tranquil reassurance. I sat on a pillow, closed my eyes, and envisioned myself in a peaceful sanctuary. That day was the first of many soul-searching encounters in the dome of crystals.

Famished and ready for a hearty meal, I headed back to the house for breakfast. A large glass of orange juice sat at each of our places. I gulped mine down and glanced expectantly toward the kitchen.

"Ja, Ja. We go now," Catharina called as she burst into the room laughing. "Straight up the mountain. Can you believe it?"

Now I understood why Catharina kept a set of cowbells on the refrigerator door. She could hear when a starving participant would raid it.

The heat was already intense by eight o'clock in the morning. We fell in line behind the drill sergeant and marched up a vertical, dusty fire trail lined with dense bushes. As I pushed myself, wheezing up the mountain, it became apparent that I was terribly out of shape. I tugged at the collar of my sweatshirt and used it to wipe the moisture off my face. I drifted in and out of a fuzzy haze as I continued hiking. Persistence was the key, putting one foot before the other, all the way to the mountain top.

Eight miles later, we staggered into the main house and collapsed on the couches. My eyes were sandy, my bones ached, and my injuries from the crash became apparent again. I glanced around at the other women and wondered if, like on them, sweat had formed dust trails down my cheeks, and if my hair was glued to my scalp. Leaning back, I fantasized about taking a cool shower as I drank a second glass of water. Then I heard the sound of Catharina's laughter and sat straight up.

"*Ja, Ja*. Time for weightlifting, ladies," Catharina said with enthusiasm. I could have strangled her, but I was too exhausted to even lift my hands. "This is Maxie, your trainer." He was a short, muscular man and like Catharina, he radiated energy. He reminded me of one of Santa's busy elves. Within minutes, we were lifting thirty-pound weights. Maxie stopped at my workout station and grinned. I detected the strong scent of garlic when he said with a slight accent, "Every day I vill increase your veights. You vill be strong and trim. Veights are the best to tone the body."

I grunted a response. I had considered myself to be about ten pounds overweight, but in fair shape. Here it was, only ten o'clock in the morning and I was on the verge of collapse. My legs felt like overcooked noodles and my arms trembled from exertion. I blinked back tears and wished my blue Mustang would show up to rescue me.

"*Ja, Ja*. Swimming pool. Ten minutes! Can you believe it?"

I sighed with relief at the thought of a relaxing dip in cool water.

Would anyone notice if I crawled into the pool with my sweats on? This was not a sunbathing splash session, I realized soon after I had put on my swimsuit. We were here to play water volleyball.

The water temperature was so cold that I wondered if it would even melt ice cubes. Wildly uncoordinated, our flailing efforts kept us from dying of hypothermia. Catharina must have thought we had recuperated because she insisted we play two games.

While enduring Catharina's regime of health and fitness exercises, I found myself trying to analyze her. Her zest for life was obviously sincere and her radiant beauty was not bought at a cosmetic counter. Perhaps if I studied her closely, I could learn her secret to happiness.

After water volleyball, we donned shapeless white robes and convened for a luncheon of cantaloupe halves garnished with a dollop of plain yogurt and all the water we could drink. We gobbled up every morsel.

"Ja, Ja."

What now, I wondered, *calisthenics in the noonday sun?*

"Massage and two-hour rest period. Sleep well, ladies."

A therapeutic massage eased the pain in my aching muscles. Oh how I wished the massage could have gone on for three more hours. I dragged myself to bed and was asleep within seconds. I was certain I'd only slept five minutes before Catharina was knocking at my door, insisting it was time to jog.

"Ja, Ja, pick up eight pebbles. Begin to jog around the track. At the end of each lap, drop a pebble into the can located beneath the large willow tree."

After four laps, I considered depositing two pebbles at a time, but my respect for the woman who was fast becoming my inspiration would not allow me to cheat. I huffed an exasperated sigh and dropped a single pebble into the can.

"Ja, you're doing great, Donna," Catharina called out, trotting past me. "Keep it up," she laughed, "just one more mile."

My overwhelming exhaustion grew by the minute, but the torture went on. Next on the agenda was a three-mile hike.

"Smile," Catharina joked. "No hills, all flat. See, an easy hike for you. Go at your own pace. It will be fun. Can you believe it?"

Now, why couldn't I believe a three-mile hike would be fun?

We returned from the hike dusty, sweaty, and beyond fatigued.

"*Ja*, ladies. Here we go! Up on the roof for aerobics."

Hearing the sound of disco music wafting down from the roof, I realized she was serious. Bleary eyed and dog-tired, I dragged myself up the steps. Too tired to even object, I shuffled through the routines like a rag doll, not caring what I looked like or whether I was in sync with the music. I noticed two of the women slouched down on a sit-down strike. I did even better. When the music stopped, I sprawled spread-eagle down on the mat.

The next thing I knew, Catharina was shaking me, tempting, "Wake up sleepyhead. I have a treat in store for you."

Ah, food, I thought.

"It is relaxation and yoga in the meditation dome."

"I can't move," I answered.

"*Ja*. You can." Catharina laughed, reached for my hands, and pulled me to my feet.

"Clear your mind of negative thoughts. Visualize yourself at your end result: healthy, active, and in good shape," she said, steering me up the path to the dome.

In spite of myself, I had to admit Catharina was right. After a day of surviving the Ashram's exhausting boot camp, yoga in the meditation dome had reduced my fatigue and I could at least walk back to the dining room without help.

Dinner that night was a huge salad. Carrots, radishes, cucumbers, tomatoes, and red peppers topped a bed of lettuce and I savored each crunchy bite. It didn't bother me in the least when we went to bed well before dark.

My greatest goal was making it through each day, and each day was much the same as the last. Only the fruits and vegetables were different. Every day the boot camp inmates' conversations focused on food—tastes, textures, colors. By the fourth day, our complaining subsided some, we lightened up, and our general attitude was more positive. We marched up the side of the mountain with one thing on our minds: losing weight. We even ate our food more slowly, enjoying each bite because we knew we weren't going to get seconds. Our disheveled hair and freedom from makeup gave us child-like happiness.

I anticipated the weigh-in at the end of the week, knowing I would have substantial results. What! The scale had to be wrong. I weighed myself four times to make sure it was accurate. I had shed only three pounds after such a grueling week. I nearly killed myself by starving and working out from sunrise to sunset and only lost three pounds! Ridiculous! Other women had lost up to ten pounds. My vision seemed hopeless. I blurted out my frustration to Catharina.

"Don't worry, Donna. You are doing fabulous! Your metabolism burns slow. *Ja*, you will lose at a slower pace. You need plenty of exercise and lots of water to increase your metabolic rate. Most important is to get your body healthy. Soon, your skin will radiate, your hair will shine, and your eyes will be so clear. It takes time to rid your body of junk food. You must replace the vitamins lost from bulimia. You are working to find your own path to health. Can you believe it?"

"Can I believe it!" I mumbled to myself as I walked away.

Patience, that's what I needed to have. Get rid of frustration and insert patience, not my strong quality. I was committed to three more weeks at the Ashram, and I didn't know if I could endure all this work with so little reward.

The next week we sat down for lunch in our orange t-shirts and sweat pants, when a new guest was introduced as a reporter from *Vogue* magazine. We stared at her in awe. She wore makeup, was glamorous, and had every lacquered hair perfectly in place. I downed my juice, polished off my tuna-stuffed papaya, and even ate the papaya skin while Miss Vogue sat across from me, watching, appalled. Two days later, I didn't blink an eye when I saw her disheveled and eating her papaya skin. That was the beauty of the Ashram.

By the end of the third week, the physical change I longed for happened. I was firm and toned, my skin wore a healthy glow, and the luster was restored to my hair. Though still tired at the end of the day, I pulled myself out of bed each morning a little faster than the day before.

In the fourth week, I was elated when my friend Brooke showed up and we became roommates. She was close to my age, vivacious, and a flight attendant. Oh yes, she was my brother's ex-wife and even though they had been divorced for years, we had a great friendship. In fact, he had remarried and was divorced again. Since Brooke had an outrageous sweet tooth, I wondered how she would survive the holistic diet.

During a scorching hot hike on the fire trail, I glanced behind and saw Brooke trudging up the trail in her orange sweat suit, looking like a wilted marigold. I remembered vividly my first days at the Ashram—pure hell, but they became easier, as they would for Brooke. I quickened my pace until I caught up to Catharina. I gave her the high sign. Jogging beside Catharina, my heart pounded, but my thighs no longer burned; my gait had turned light-footed and steady. I glanced at her face aglow with serenity and it seemed the right time to ask what had been on my mind since my arrival.

"What makes you so happy?"

She stopped jogging, sat down on a nearby rock, and gestured for me to sit next to her. We each took a moment to catch our breath and have a cool drink of water before she said, "Donna, don't you know yet? No one thing or person can make you happy. Only you can bring happiness to yourself. *Ja.*"

I glanced over at her and sighed in exasperation. "I've heard that before, but what does it mean? How do I make me happy? I can't give myself acting jobs."

Catharina bowed her head and smiled. "First, learn who you are. Many people come here only to get in shape. One needs awareness of spirit and the power of body working together on all levels." She motioned her finger at me. "But you cannot let the outer control the inner. *Ja?*"

"And how do I do that?" I questioned.

Catharina nodded. "For almost a month, I have watched you. Don't ever be afraid to show the real you." She rose and started back up the trail, calling over her shoulder, "Truth lies behind all things. Find it, but do not judge yourself. Let yourself be."

As I followed Catharina up the mountain, with two strides to each one of hers, I pondered over what she had said. George had said the exact same thing: learn to love and accept yourself. I was working on it but it still eluded me.

That night, a full moon brightened the sky above the Ashram. My introspective mood lingered and I couldn't sleep. I stared at the clock, watching the second hand make its jerky revolution, and recalled hurtful memories from long ago. Thinking back to those troubled days always started my insides churning. I finally gave up on sleep and climbed out of bed. I moved quietly down the stairs and headed for the main room. Sitting on the sofa, I was contemplating the message above the fireplace when I heard soft footsteps in the kitchen. The jangle of cow bells meant only one thing: the refrigerator door was being opened. I jumped up and peeked around the doorway in time to see Catharina running down the stairs and heading for the kitchen. Whoever was raiding the refrigerator was asking for a tongue-lashing.

"Brookie! Brookie! What are you doing, Brookie? I want to know. Are you eating something?" Catharina asked in a commanding voice.

I crept to the door of the kitchen and heard Brooke's muffled response, "Umph, umph-uh." Shaking my head while smiling, I understood that her sweet tooth had gotten the best of her.

The neon ceiling light came on and Catharina zeroed in. "What do you have in your mouth, Brookie? Are you eating the staff's leftover birthday cake?"

"Umph-uh." Brooke stood in the doorway, cheeks bulging like a chipmunk, shaking her head vigorously. Then she made a dash for the bathroom and slammed the door shut behind her. Soon afterward, I heard the toilet flush.

Catharina stood outside the bathroom door with her arms crossed. "Brookie," she called, "the cake is down the toilet?"

After a few seconds of Brooke's silence, Catharina turned and walked into the main room where I was sitting and eyed me suspiciously. "Donna, were you eating cake too?" Though only seen by moonlight, something in my eyes must have prompted her to say, "No. I think you were after something else. What were you doing here sitting by yourself?"

"Can't sleep. Since our conversation today, I keep thinking about my family."

"What about them?" she asked softly.

"They have influenced so many of my decisions. I love my family, and I believe they love me, each in their own way, but it always bothered me that praise, or even a compliment, was such a rarity in our household. I assumed I wasn't worthy or good enough. In the days before the plane crash, I had zero self-worth and actually had a death wish. When I think back, I took the path of least resistance and wound up on the road to self-destruction." I shook my head. "I don't want to go there ever again."

Catharina placed her hand on my arm. "You don't have to. What you have learned from your past and what you believe today can alter your future."

"I have to heal the past or at least understand it if I plan on a promising future. My parents' divorce was one drama after another as I struggled with the hatred between them. My mother filed for divorce when I was in the hospital with malnutrition. I don't think my father ever forgave me for that. Sounds strange, but there was not enough food to eat in our house. Maybe that's why I hold on to an extra ten or fifteen pounds now, like having fat in the bank. Let me get back on track. The interesting part of the story is that I was in a state of not being able to stay conscious for very long, and then after two weeks, surges of energy bolted through my body and I felt good. Wow, I can still recall that."

Catharina was listening but she said nothing.

"My parents never spoke one word to each other from that day forward. I was left to interpret for myself what the communication between them was. Which parent would I upset on holidays, which always turned into battlefields anyway? I could only spend the holiday with one, and since they didn't talk I had to make the choice. Then I had to live with the wrath of the other parent. I was the pawn in the middle. Up until I was eighteen, I had to spend every weekend with my father, by court order. The legal battles were unbelievably ugly; my brother and I had to go to court more than a dozen times." I stopped to collect my thoughts because there was a part of me that didn't want to think about the past.

"Continue," Catharina said softly.

"I worked diligently on my ski race training, trying to come back after my heart catheterization operation the year before. Snow skiing was how I alleviated my frustration. On the way to my father's house to attend ski practice, the car broke down three times and I was late. I walked in, and he began hitting me again and again. When he finally stopped his raging, I ran to my bedroom and burrowed in a corner of the closet. My body was bruised and throbbing. My ribs felt like they were broken. I crouched there for hours, agonizing over my dream. If I stayed with my father, I had a chance at the Olympics, my dream come true. I had trained relentlessly for eight years. If I left and became my own person, the goal I had worked for would vanish. I didn't have the money to travel and compete, and my mother couldn't afford it either. After hours of vacillating, I walked out the door and understood I would rather stand on my own two feet and be alone than be controlled.

"I understand," Catharina said in a whisper.

"Now that I am talking about this, there is a side note. My father insisted I have the heart surgery in the first place. My mother felt we should monitor it longer and be sure. He attempted to sue her for neglect, so to stop the fighting I agreed to have the catheterization. I didn't even know what was involved; I just couldn't tolerate another court battle. My father drove me to Philadelphia, about an hour and a half from home, dropped me off at the hospital, and left me to meet the doctors and nurses and go through the operation by myself. He said he had business and would be back in a week after the surgery to take me home. He threatened my mother in writing, insisting that if she visited me he would take her back to court. In a different city, with doctors I had never seen before, I was prepped for major surgery. During the three-hour operation I was kept semi-awake, and I suddenly heard the doctors yelling that they were losing me. Then I felt strange surges of energy bolt through my body. It was gone. I felt peaceful. It was the same energy I had encountered when I had malnutrition. Unbelievable.

"My brother arrived home from college and my mother gave him about an hour to rest, and then had him drive to the hospital during my recovery to make sure I was okay because she was frantic with worry. I was elated when I could leave the hospital. My father dropped me off at my mother's house and I carried in my suitcase by myself and spent most of my time consoling her, insisting I was fine. Now, when I say it out loud, I realize I didn't spend any time healing me."

I wrapped my arms around my chest to ward off the chill I felt.

Catharina said, "Go on."

" I ... I ... I don't understand why I didn't comprehend this earlier, but I picked men—and trust me, I dated a lot, and I mean a lot, and even had marriage proposals too—but I chose men who disappointed me and were not there for me when I needed them. Interesting!"

Catharina said softly, "Donna, go on and get it out. *Ja.*"

I nodded as I felt my eyes swell up with tears. "After the beating, when I gave up my skiing career, I didn't visit my father and I lived at my mother's full time. It was only a few months until I turned eighteen and the court order would end. I knew Mom truly loved me, and that her heart was in the right place. She always accepted my friends into our home and made sure they were fed. We had a fantastic vegetable garden in our back yard.

"She meant well; she was just tough at times. Once, while trying on clothes, I pirouetted out of the dressing room wearing a lovely brown pant suit. 'Oh yes, you should wear that; it's dark and doesn't make you look fat,' she declared in her most helpful tone.

'"Mother, this is a size ten. I diet, and even throw up to be thin. Can't you say I look good?'

"Astonished, my mother asked, 'You mean you throw up your food?'

'Yes,' I answered, and hung my head.

'"Well, throwing up isn't doing you any good; you're still fat.'"

I started to rock back and forth, feeling ill at ease. Catharina placed her arm around me and pushed back my hair.

Grabbing a pillow and holding it over my stomach, I glanced at Catharina. "I desperately wanted to get along with my family, and even gave my father another chance. This was the one that really did it for me. At the end of my second year at the University of Montana, he called and told me if I spent time with him during the summer, he would pay for my tuition for the upcoming year. Even with his history of broken promises, I wanted to believe him. I was transferring to the University of Hawaii for my junior year and I was so excited. It was all I talked about that summer. Shortly before leaving for Hawaii, my tuition check came to my mom's house in the mail. He could have given it to me. My father lived in the same town. My mother had repeatedly warned me not to count on his help. I tore open the envelope and glared at the check in disbelief, fighting back waves of anger because the check was made out to the University of Montana. It was nothing but a useless piece of paper, and my father knew it. Tears of disappointment welled up and rolled down my cheeks. Running out of the house at the speed of a race horse, my feet hit the sidewalk cement and pain shot straight up my legs as I screamed, 'He will never betray me again!'"

Fighting for composure I continued, "In my mind my father was not my father. At that moment I designated my stepdad, John, as my dad. It was John who really cared. I called my father's office but was told he was away on a business trip. I wrote on the front of the check as I said it out loud, 'I am going to the University of Hawaii,' and mailed it back. My father never reissued the check; he tricked me again. He had no intention of paying for college. I wound up selling pots and pans door-to-door in Hawaii to pay for my education."

All this time, Catharina sat quietly listening to me pour my heart out. I turned to her and said, "How do you believe you're worthy enough to be loved by anyone?"

Catharina thought for a moment, then deduced, "Your virtue lies in having the faith and courage to overcome the difficulties in life. Love yourself and know you are worthy, or you won't feel worthy of another."

She held my hands and squeezed them. "Begin your healing from within. Create your own love, your own life, and surround yourself with people who love and accept you. Be with God."

I gazed intently at this woman, a living example of what I wanted to become. "I feel more sad than anything else. I don't want to transfer my parents' negative patterns to my children."

"That's good; just because your parents couldn't express their love for you in the way you wanted doesn't mean you can't demonstrate genuine love to a child someday." A warm smile spread over Catharina's face as she added, "You are replacing an unhealthy lifestyle with healthy behavior. It will take some time."

Catharina put her arms around me and gave me an incredibly comforting hug. When she pulled away, she gazed at me with a serious expression, ordering, "Clean all the confusion and doubt from your mind. Each day, say to yourself: I am worthy, I am strong, I am love."

"I thought I came to the Ashram to fix my body, but I guess I came here to fix my soul," I concluded as the tears gently rolled down my face. "I pray that someday I will be able to heal with my family."

She looked at me intensely. "Someday. *Ja*, someday you will." Catharina suppressed a yawn. "Get some sleep now; I am going to bed after I check on Brookie. I wonder if she is still spitting out chocolate cake?"

It was my turn to smile. On the way back to my room, I thought about what Catharina had said and realized she had given me the answer. For weeks I had studied her, envied her, and wondered what her secret was. Now, I knew. She lived in harmony with herself.

The next was our final day at the Ashram, I dressed in my skirt and fitted top and was overjoyed at how loosely they fit. I liked how my body felt. My skin had a radiant glow. My eyes were clear and sparkled. Outstanding—I liked this person!

Catharina waited in the driveway to congratulate us and send us on our way. When it came time for me, she grinned. "You did it, Donna. You are beautiful. I see an inner strength you didn't have when you arrived. Believe it. *Ja.*"

"Thank you," I said, heartened by her words. "I couldn't have done it without you, Catharina."

She threw up her hands protesting, "No, I didn't do it. You did. I was only your guide."

Smiling, I hugged her tightly. Before getting in the car I took a final look at the grounds, the unique meditation dome, and the rustic main house. I gazed past the open door leading to the living room. Only the last line of the wooden sign was visible over the fireplace. I beamed knowingly at my assignment. **Be.**

 Journal
One More Mile

The past is not where you should waste
your precious time on this earth
Focus on the now

Who would have thought I'd learn to enjoy hiking straight up a dirt mountain. Catharina, my drill sergeant and laughing saint, is my inspiration. I'm starting to understand that life is all about one more mile. Every day, every week, every year, just one more mile, one more lesson ... one more thing to conquer. Not only did my body glow with health from the Ashram, but also my SPIRIT. Catharina helped me understand that the past is part of who I am, but it was time to let go and to write my own script. That is a tall order. Seriously, I need to know that I am worthy on all levels and that includes all the way to my core.

Raimund and Catharina had the same message: LIVE IN THE MOMENT. I have to laugh because when hiking up the mountain, all I could think about was whether I could make the next step. Physical exercise has a way of keeping my soul in the present.

I'm on a path that I cannot turn away from. It is my spiritual journey. I am so appreciative I could spend a month at the Ashram to rid my body of toxins and open my spirit to all possibilities. I am thankful to be alive!

Chapter Seven

Time to Change

There are no accidents
everything happens for a reason
Once you understand your learning lessons
you can move to the next level

I was in my dimly lit apartment with my journal on my lap. Reaching over to the nightstand I hesitantly picked up the blaring phone and heard George's familiar voice boom, "Hi, Partner. I'm only in town another day. Where have you been?"

I blurted, "George, George. When do I get to see you?"

"I've been calling you for the last couple of days."

"Boy, I have a lot to tell you. I got back in town tonight. Hey, you never call this late, what's up?"

"Donna, I want to see you before I fly out. How about getting together for our usual 6 AM breakfast tomorrow morning?"

Ashram time, I thought. "Sure, that's fine, George," I said without my customary complaining. "Are you staying at your usual hotel?"

After a long pause, he said, "Yep. Okay, great."

"Since your hotel is only eight blocks from my apartment, I'll jog down and meet you."

"You? Jog? At six o'clock in the morning?"

I laughed, explaining, "Hey, I know it's hard for you to understand, but I had the most incredible experience this last month and well, never mind. I'll tell you all about it in the morning."

Dressed in running shoes and sweats, I jogged to the hotel, admiring the fiery glow of a crimson sunrise. After a two-armed bear hug in the coffee shop, George stood back to observe me, announcing, "You look wonderful. What have you done to yourself?"

"That's what I want to tell you," I said, grinning. "I thought wonderful was on the outside. First it was the plane crash; then it was Raimund, my guide when I went heli-skiing; and then I spent an incredible month with Catharina, at the Ashram. I discovered from her that wonderful happens on the inside. They all told me the same thing. Live in the moment. I know now you get your lessons over and over again until you understand them. Because I was open to change, teachers came into my life to guide me."

"Oh boy, let's order some food first," George said with a chuckle. "Something tells me it's going to be one of those conversations." We sat down at a table by the window. When the waitress came, George ordered coffee and for me, herbal tea.

"I do know you have been telling me the same things for years, but I needed to experience it."

After the waitress delivered our breakfast, George squinted over his plate of ham and eggs and made a face at my fruit and granola. "You know, there sure is something different going on with you."

"Mr. Miracle Worker, I have had some miracles myself. You won't believe this incredible woman I met, Catharina, and where I spent the last month." Explaining my daily routine at the Ashram, I watched George wince a few times. "Oh, I hated it when I first got there; I thought I wouldn't live through the first couple of days. Pain, pain, and more pain is what my body felt. When it was time to go home I didn't want to leave. Is that crazy or what?"

George seemed amused as he took another bite of food. "I would have hated it at the beginning and hated it at the end."

"Well, I guess it's not for everyone," I chuckled. "The more I learned about loving and accepting myself, the easier each day became. It was sort of like a magical transformation." Up to this point, George had remained pretty quiet and had let me ramble on. "So, what do you think about all this?" I asked while sipping my tea.

He pushed his empty plate aside and fished out his pipe and tobacco pouch. "It's funny how you find the truth when you least expect it."

George paused from packing tobacco into his pipe. "Most folks won't admit that hanging on to the past is a weakness. It takes a lot of work to put the past where it belongs. To imagine a new beginning without the old can be pretty intimidating. Remember this: there are no accidents; everything happens for a reason. Once you understand you're learning lessons you can move to the next level."

"Glad you said that. Ready for this next shocker?"

"What? Now what have you been up to?"

"Not what I have been up to. It is what I am about to do." He stared at me. "Here we go: I'm leaving Los Angeles. I can't believe it. I've decided to move to Lake Tahoe. I love the mountains. Every time I go there to snow ski I feel alive."

George slightly raised an eyebrow muttering, "I see."

"Hey, I'm being forced to move. My apartment building has been sold to a developer. He insisted we move out in a month. I fought the owner and won; he was not happy but he gave the tenants a six-month extension—still, I have to move. I've made phone calls and checked out at over a dozen apartments, but there always seems to be something wrong. Moving to Tahoe means giving up being an actress and finding a new career. Sure I act, but to fill in and make ends meet

I've sold boats, motor homes, pictures, plants, and real estate. Now, that's a checkered past. It's a massive change for me to move, and unsettling. The developer and I had many heated discussions. He called later and offered me a job because he wanted me on his side. He was insistent I never relocate to any of his buildings again. Los Angeles is now going to be in my past. Amazing! Did I say that?"

George looked intently at me. "Leaving Los Angeles. Hmmm. Interesting. Time for a change. Yes, time for a big change—I think it will be good for you."

I took a sip of my tea and waited for more. "This is important. Do you have any insight as to how I'll earn my living?"

George tucked his tobacco pouch into his pocket and held his unlit pipe in his hand. He took a deep breath and his eyes glazed over with a faraway look. After a while he turned to me, proclaiming, "You're going to talk."

"I meant, what will I do for a career?"

"What do you do best?"

"Huh?"

"Talk. That's what you do best and it's going to be your career." He glanced at his watch and pushed back his chair. "I'm sorry, Partner, but I have to go. I have an eight o'clock meeting; we'll talk more about this another time."

"Promise?" It was like George not to reveal too much too soon. He had planted the seed of suggestion and would wait to see what I would do with it.

"I promise."

I picked up the check and giggled with delight. "I really have changed. I'm buying, George, breakfast is on me!"

 Journal
Time to Change

***When one door closes
another one opens***

George, what a bonus to see him. His timing is uncanny. The sight of him makes me happy. Thanks to my days at the Ashram I didn't mind getting up before sunrise. That was a shocker to George. The good news is he noticed there is something different about me. There was a more positive energy around me. Even when I told him I was moving to Tahoe, he seemed to understand it was time to alter my path. When I asked him what I would do he said I would talk ... what exactly did he mean by that? Talk to people, sell, what?

Universe, I understand how important it is to keep healing, but the reality is I have to get back to work and create a living. A little cash would help—no, let me restate that: a lot of cash would help. I am moving from Los Angeles, which I never thought I would do, and into a new career. Career—even the word is unsettling. Now is the time for me to make a CHANGE. I am scared!

I ask the question: How do I determine the work I will love and know it will be right for me? The only thing I can think of is ... MASSIVE CHANGE.

Chapter Eight

Manifest Your Passion

Make work your passion

Glancing down at the Pacific Ocean, I wondered where the past few years had gone. Living in Tahoe had not been as fulfilling as I had imagined. Home was a bunk bed at my brother's ski cabin; work consisted of serving cocktails and selling jewelry, which really didn't qualify as a career move. Men in my life were nowhere to be found. Finally, I was hired by a modeling agency in Reno to teach students how to interview for television commercials. Then, one of the parents was so impressed with how I motivated the teenagers that he asked me to train his employees concerning attitude. One thing led to another and I developed a workshop called *Is Your Attitude Showing?* Next, I started speaking about how to have an attitude adjustment, manage stress, and communicate clearly. I began each presentation describing how the plane accident altered my outlook in a matter of seconds. Slowly, I built a name for myself. Now I was flying to Hawaii to present the biggest speech of my life.

The airline pilot announced that the flight attendants should prepare for our arrival in Honolulu. I adjusted my seat back and tightened my seat belt. Sudden turbulence jostled the plane, and I gripped the armrests. Fear spun wildly through my mind and my heart raced. A haunting vision flashed before me: an aircraft on fire, people burning, screams of pain, and stunned survivors huddled in groups. Beads of sweat formed on my forehead. Seconds dragged on before I loosened my grip on the armrests and tried to regulate my breathing. Forcing the horrific images from my mind, I focused on a safe landing on the tarmac in Hawaii. During the years since the plane crash, my anxiety attacks happened less frequently, but I never knew when a flashback would occur. Whenever I flew, my nerves were still jittery. I took deep breaths to calm myself and glanced out the window. The aircraft swooped over the brilliant blues of the Oahu coast. I gazed down on Diamond Head and the sight of palm trees and breaking waves on the white sandy beaches beckoning. The scene transported me back to the nostalgic magic of the islands. I was coming home. Hawaii had its hold on me. Yes, I was a former Miss Hawaii—not by blood but by spirit. Hawaii soothed my soul; there was a connection, maybe in the distant past.

I felt a slight jolt on touchdown, and beamed as the aircraft made a safe landing. Coming down the ramp I inhaled the sweet scent of plumeria and felt the warm, tropical sea breeze like silk against my skin.

When the taxi dropped me off at my hotel in Waikiki, I pinched myself several times. When I first came to the Hawaiian Islands, I was a college student who sold pots and pans to pay my tuition at the University of Hawaii. I had no money and lived on rice, pineapple, guava, and coconuts. Through determination and persistence, I won the title of Miss Hawaii. Then, moving to the Colony Surf at Diamond Head, every night I fell asleep to the sound of the ocean. Hawaii will always be an enchanted paradise for me. It bolstered my confidence like nowhere else on earth.

I had barely enough time to check into my room and freshen up before meeting with my former cookware boss, Chuck Smart, a man whose name always brought a smile to my face. Casually dressed in white pants and a sleeveless blue shell, I walked the short distance to a local favorite, the Tahitian Lanai. The atmosphere was grass hut dining, with tables arranged around an oval swimming pool. Chuck saw me right away and flagged me over. One would have to be sightless to overlook this big, powerfully built man. He had chiseled features, dark hair, and chestnut eyes that brimmed with enthusiasm.

"How's my 'Dynamite Donna' doing?" he shouted, his big arms encircling me.

"Great, Chuck, and how is the king of pots and pans?"

He grinned. "Well, you gotta eat, so you gotta cook. Pots and pans are outstanding."

He took my arm and steered me into one of the little Tahitian huts. I said, "I'm impressed, Chuck. These huts are always reserved way ahead of time."

He shot me one of his famous winks. "I reserved this hut especially for Miss Hawaii."

Dressed in a long floral muumuu, the waitress stopped at the table to take our order. After she left, I grinned across the table at Chuck, thinking how tan and healthy he appeared. His strong traits were that he was an easy conversationalist and generous with his advice regarding people skills—a salesman through and through. Our drinks arrived with a tray of Hawaiian appetizers called *pupus* by the islanders. As we nibbled Chuck inquired, "So now that you've moved away from Hollywood, how do you like living in Tahoe?"

"I love it; Tahoe is magical. The area is famous for incredible skiing, beautiful weather, and the magnificent clear lake. I'm renting a bed in my brother's mountain home with 13 other skiers. It's a little crowded on weekends but I guess I should consider myself lucky since I have the top bunk. This starting-over stuff is interesting."

Chuck raised one dark fly-away brow. "Right. Why there? I thought you were a warm weather gal."

"I still like warm weather, but I'm addicted to skiing. When I was in junior high school I attended the 1960 Olympics in Squaw Valley, California with my father and brother. What an unforgettable experience it was, with the most rugged, outrageous mountain I had ever skied. At the base of the mountain, I visited a little church with stained glass windows and prayed I would someday live in Tahoe. Twenty years later, I moved there."

Chuck laughed. "Dream it and it'll happen."

"That's exactly why I'm here." I leaned forward. "I have a dream and I want to make it happen."

"Okay, Dynamite Donna. Let's hear it."

Pausing to figure out where to begin, after a moment I said, "I came to Hawaii to speak at a conference. I'm working at becoming more comfortable with public speaking, but I know nothing about running my own business. I don't have much money, but I know what I want to do. I've been serving drinks to make ends meet in Tahoe." I leveled my index finger at my head. "Me, who doesn't know a Manhattan from a Martini. I kept putting olives in drinks that needed cherries." I chuckled. "The only thing I know about cocktails is in Hawaii they're served either on fire or with an umbrella on top."

Chuck tried to restrain himself but then convulsed with laughter. "You never were much for the hard stuff."

"I started working in Reno, coaching teenagers who wanted to do commercials. One of the parents asked me to speak to his small group of employees on attitude and customer service . From there, I went on to speak for larger companies. You know, my mentor George told me I would talk for a living. Hindsight is underrated, because when I went to college I only got one 'A' and it was in ... speaking. I should have figured this out sooner. Chuck, your help please. You've been running a successful business for as long as I've known you and I need your expert advice."

Chuck leaned in close and his dark brows merged at the bridge of his nose. I remembered that same intense look when he wanted to make a point during our cookware meetings. "Let's start with when you first came to work for me," he said. "You were a college student, you had to pay fifteen dollars for a bond to sell pots and pans, and your check bounced."

I protested, "I was broke."

"Donna, did you sell any cookware that first month?"

"Your memory is too good. No, I didn't sell any cookware." I leaned back in my chair and stared down at my hands.

"Why not?"

Sighing, I recalled, "I thought it was beneath me to knock on doors and sell pots and pans. Didn't like doing it, my friends made fun of me, and I felt my parents should be paying for my education. Bad attitude." Turning away from his searching eyes, I continued, "Yes, you did what any boss would do. You fired me."

After a moment, Chuck said, "I did what I had to do."

"I know. But I came back to talk to you later that day with tears streaming down my cheeks and pleaded for my job back." Smiling at the memory, I said, "Thanks for giving me another shot at it."

He laughed. "I knew you had it in you all along, kid. You needed direction and an attitude adjustment." He smiled and reached for another coconut shrimp.

"After you hired me back, you took me out on sales calls for training. Having you there boosted my confidence and ..."

"Hang on a minute. Let's not get ahead of ourselves," Chuck interrupted, cocking his head inquisitively. "That day when you came back after I fired you, what changed your mind about selling cookware?"

"I had to. I had no money!"

Chuck smiled. "I'd say that's a valid reason. At first, you listened to other people who weren't thinking of your best interest. You had to learn to stop listening to bad advice."

I flashed him a questioning look.

"You'll get all kinds of advice. Pay close attention to who is giving you that counsel, and let your instincts tell you if that person truly has your best interest at heart. Okay. What happened to you then?" Chuck asked with a wry smile crossing his face.

"Living and breathing cookware, I became one of the highest ranking sales people in the United States. Not bad for someone who got fired. Yep, I even won scholarships to the University of Hawaii. Amazing ... from selling cookware."

"That's right. It was a perfect job for you at the time. You had a real passion for what you did. You liked running a sales crew and coming to meetings, when you weren't late from surfing." I rolled my eyes. "What else spurred you on?" he asked, his enthusiasm bubbling up.

"The camaraderie, the recognition, the opportunity to feel like a winner, and the product. Hey, the cookware is guaranteed for a lifetime; I still use it every day."

"Oh yeah. You bet! You have to believe in what you're doing," Chuck boomed as he pounded the table top to emphasize his point.

"That's why I want to speak, but how do I keep it going? I don't have pots and pans to sell. I just have me."

Chuck's eyes widened. "Oh? What's wrong with you? You have to have passion, Dynamite Donna. Back in those days, I saw the potential in you, but you didn't." He paused and inhaled deeply. "Let me give you a few more tips to help you figure it out. Recall when I had you write out your sales goals each week?"

"Yes, of course. I was afraid I wouldn't reach them."

Chuck continued, "You reached your goals many times. So why don't you do that now? Write down your goals and map out where you want to be, in a month, three months, six months, and a year from now. What kind of lifestyle do you want? How much money do you want to make? How do you want to give back to others? And don't forget to make time for the fun things."

"Yes, I like the fun part," I kidded.

"Next, get organized. If you're working for yourself, you have to set guidelines and stick by them. Make a schedule and live by it. What time to get up, when to start work, how many calls to make each day, and most importantly, time for follow-up."

"Okay. What else?" I asked, excited by the idea of purposeful planning.

He continued with the same electric energy he used when presenting at our cookware meetings. "When people work for themselves, their greatest cause of failure is not managing their time effectively. Don't let procrastination steal your time."

"I know all about that," I said.

"Donna, you know how this works. Think back to that Christmas Eve when it was the deadline for the company's scholarship contest and all you needed was one more sale."

"Oh, yes. I called you to say I was out on sales calls and getting turned down left and right. I was afraid I wouldn't make it."

"That's right. Then, you ran across a serviceman on leave from Vietnam who hadn't bought his wife anything for Christmas. Cookware was the solution. When you called, I asked you—"

I interrupted, "You asked me what I was doing selling cookware so late on Christmas Eve. Actually, I was supposed to be at a luau with friends, but I didn't go because I desperately needed that scholarship."

Chuck laughed. "That's what I call managing your time. You prioritized, got the sale, made the deadline, and won the scholarship."

I took a sip of juice and said, "Uh-huh, and he was really cute too."

"Who?"

"My date, Eddie. I caught up with him after the luau."

Chuck gave me a fatherly glare. "Right. So, you had some good times too. You know how to prioritize, Dynamite Donna. Now, you've got some work ahead of you. Figure out your goals, get organized, and be persistent." Chuck grinned and continued, "I'm a risk taker, a betting man, and I'd bet on you."

As darkness closed in on the pinkish glow of the sunset, Chuck drove me to my hotel.

"I can always count on you," I said gratefully, giving him a kiss on the cheek and squeezing his hand.

Later that night in my room, I thought more about our conversation. It occurred to me what a powerful person my pot and pan boss was in my life. I had disliked selling cookware in the beginning, but he taught me to provide for myself and be passionate about what I wanted. I was blessed to have crossed paths with this motivated man.

Waking at dawn the next morning I dressed in shorts, rented a bicycle, and headed for a peaceful little refuge that overlooked the ocean. The ride to Diamond Head was uplifting and my body responded to the vigorous workout. When I caught sight of my favorite flat boulder, I jumped off my bike and leaned it against a palm tree. Sitting down, I took a few moments to relax, then closed my eyes and began to meditate. The sound of breaking waves and the warm sun on my back had a calming effect.

I opened my eyes to a cluster of surfers paddling out to catch their first waves, reminding me of my college days when I would be out riding the waves at sunrise. I'd surf the early morning hours and quit barely in time to attend my cookware meeting and then dash up to the University with a minute to spare before class. It wasn't unusual for me to show up with wet hair and bare feet. I loved to surf. I wanted to feel that exhilaration again but it would have to wait; I had a luncheon date.

Breathlessly arriving back at the hotel, I changed into a flowered cotton dress and walked from Waikiki to the Ala Moana Shopping

Center. I passed the pond of carp and the little bookstore where Dr. Bob had taken me to buy self-help books. Dr. Robert Gibson was a well-known local dentist, but to me, he was always Dr. Bob.

While competing for the title of Miss Hawaii, I needed my teeth capped and the best referral was Dr. Bob. He had a brilliant reputation and a price tag to match. A philanthropist at heart, he was an aloha-type friendly man with a black mustache and an endearing stutter. The first time I met him, I settled back in his chair with my mouth wide open as he prodded and poked, saying, "Uh-huh ... we'll move this ... redo these four teeth ... oh, yes ... perfect! Y-y-y-you will be marvelous when we're d-d-done."

When his receptionist added up the total cost for all the work to be done, it was my turn to stutter. "H-h-how much?" I stammered. I thought the price was outrageous, but I returned every week for three months with my cookware earnings to pay the bill. Each week, Dr. Bob would give me a different self-help book to read. During the following visits, busy as he was, he always took the time to discuss the book with me. My teeth turned out gorgeous, the work of a real perfectionist. What I didn't know at the time was that he was not only changing my outside appearance, but improving me from the inside as well. That was Dr. Bob's greatest gift.

The Ala Moana Professional Building was right next door to the shopping center. I took the elevator to the top floor where the revolving restaurant offered its customers a spectacular view of Honolulu. The maitre d' pointed me in the direction of Dr. Bob's booth and there he was, punctual as ever, already waiting.

When I sat down, he covered my hand with his, greeting, "Aloha. Wonderful to s-s-see you, Donna. I don't have much t-t-time so I took the liberty of ordering a papaya lunch for us."

I grinned and exclaimed, "I love papaya!"

Making small talk, we caught up on the latest news during lunch. As we finished, Dr. Bob became serious. "When you c-c-called me a few days ago, you said it was absolutely important that we meet. What's this all about?"

"I'm here in Hawaii to do a presentation for a group of top executives, but I'm new to the speaking profession and I am open to suggestions. Remember when you gave me all those self-help books and how reading them inspired me? Well, that's what I want to do when I speak. I met with my former cookware boss last night and have a better idea of how to organize my business, and I'd like to ask for your input as well."

Dr. Bob enthusiastically answered, "I understand. I'm going to give you t-t-two pearls of wisdom. First, no matter how many presentations you give, keep taking classes, attending workshops, and reading inspirational books. Invest in yourself. Stretch your mind. There is no limit to s-s-self-improvement. You are who you believe you are."

He sat back and sighed. "The second little pearl is always go to the top."

"Okay, I understand about the books, but what do you mean by 'go to the top'?"

Dr. Bob furrowed his brow for a moment. "When you need help with accounting, marketing, or whatever, go to the t-t-top people and ask for advice because that's where you want to position yourself, at the top." He glanced at his watch. "Now I must get back d-d-down to my office."

Having an insightful realization, I blurted out, "Dr. Bob, you don't just fix teeth; you fix lives."

He was quiet for a beat. "Well, some of both." He reached down on the seat and pulled up a book. "I saw this in the bookstore and thought you might like it."

I chuckled when I saw the cover. "Outstanding! It's the same book I saw in the window on the way over here."

"By the way, there's a phone message tucked inside the cover.

Someone c-c-called my office looking for you. Every time you arrive back in the islands and your name appears in the 'who's who' column of the newspaper, people start calling my office looking for you."

"Thanks for the book and for being my answering service. People seem to know I always look you up when I come to Hawaii. You are the best."

After saying goodbye, I unfolded the message. *I'm overdue for one of those flaming volcano drinks. I'm in Hawaii. Join me at the Hilton Hawaiian Village at eight o'clock tonight, George.* Delighted, I thought, *George is here in Hawaii! Wonderful! This is my day. I'll even have time to go surfing before meeting him.* I was itching to surf, but realized I hadn't written in my journal the last couple of nights. I could quickly jot down some of the ideas given to me by Chuck and Dr. Bob. Almost jogging back to my hotel, and barely missing a skateboarder, I started to organize my thoughts.

Journal
Manifest Your Passion

Always keep learning

When I first started selling pots and pans, I thought it was the worst job in the world. Little did I know that the sales strategies I learned then would be the exact same ones I would use today in my speaking career. Funny how life comes full circle. When I look back on those years of hawking cookware, I understand how that experience taught me focus and self-motivation. So, here's what I need to do. Manage my time, set a schedule, get organized, write down my goals, and then stick to my plan on a daily basis.

Then, there's Dr. Bob. I never thought a dentist would be such a pivotal force in my life. He offered me two pearls of wisdom. NEVER STOP LEARNING and go to the top.

Okay Universe, I'm making this short. It's surfing time. Thank you for putting the right people in my path to teach me. I am grateful to be back in Hawaii with a surfboard underfoot. Oh no, can I still surf?

Chapter Nine

Ride the Wave

Face your fears
Push past them

The waves at Diamond Head were breaking at about three feet. It had been a long while since I surfed with the locals and the thought of riding a breaking wave had me exploding with excitement. An unexpected wave pressed me into action, but my reaction wasn't quick enough. There was no time to flip my board over and wrap my feet around it. The wave battered me, pulling the surfboard from my arms and forcing me to swim back to the beach to retrieve it. Surfing requires balance and timing and I had to get my rhythm back. My arms were trembling from exertion as I carried the board back from the sandy beach into the ocean.

Let's try this again. I got about halfway out to the breakers when another wave came along and ripped my board from my hands. I repeated the same process of swimming back to the beach to retrieve my board. Standing in ankle-deep water, my arms were numb and I could feel the blazing sun scorching my back. This was not what I expected. Instead of gracefully riding the waves to shore, I was being slammed around like a rodeo clown on a bucking bronco.

I don't know why I kept paddling back out. Could it be that I am bullheaded? Finally, I made it past the breakers and sat on the surfboard waiting for a wave. Hard as I tried, I miscalculated five of them. Embarrassed, I glanced around at the sun-bronzed locals and sensed their mocking stares. Under my breath I mumbled, "Donna you're the only pale-faced, red-haired *haole* female out here." Then one of the locals broke away from the line and paddled over.

He sported a grin, asking, "Ey rough day?"

"Believe it or not," I said, all flustered, "I used to surf all the time, but I've been away for a couple of years." Then I thought to myself, *Actually, a lot more than a couple.*

He nodded. "Hmmm. Too anxious. Kick back. Get one with wave."

"You're right." It had been some time since I'd heard the local pidgin slang. "That must be it; I'm too anxious."

"Ey. Loosen up. You live here?"

"No, not anymore, but I did graduate from the University of Hawaii."

"Ey. You gonna be here awhile ... maybe surf again?"

"I'm here for a couple of days. I might come out again. Apparently I could use the practice."

He smiled and winked. "See you tomorrow. We get together."

The surfer swiveled his head and said, "Ey. That's your wave. You catch it."

Just before it crested, I paddled like crazy. Ecstatic, I stood on the board, adjusted my feet, balanced my body, made sure my knees were bent, and rode it to shore. When I glimpsed back at the ocean I understood my lesson was not to force life. Hadn't I learned that before?

Riding the waves until I was depleted, I glanced at the line of surfers and this time the locals gave me a thumbs up.

My newfound friend paddled over, complimenting, "Ey. You no talk story. You really surf."

I beamed, and caught the next wave to shore where I hooked the surfboard on my hip, turned, and gave my surfer buddy a nod. Taking a deep breath, I glanced up at Diamond Head, lifted my surfboard on top of my head, and started the steep climb.

Back at my hotel, I felt exhilarated but exhausted. Desperately needing a shower and a nap, I decided the first thing to do was leave George a message telling him he would be seeing my smiling face at eight.

Arriving on time at the Hilton Hawaiian Village, I went directly to the beachside bar to find George. Scanning the crowd I heard, "Hey Partner!" There he was, sitting at a table beneath the Tiki torches, sporting a yellow and red Hawaiian shirt and smoking his blooming pipe.

He beckoned, "Get over here. I need my volcano drink right now, before I erupt."

I hugged George, sat down, and joyfully asserted, "What a surprise. How do you always show up when I need you?"

Before he could answer, the waiter took our order. As he left, George said, "I'm here because I got a call from a client in Honolulu who needed me. The only way to knock some sense into him was to talk to the guy in person, so I caught the first flight out, and here I am. Last time we talked you said you'd be here now, so I called Dr. Bob."

"Oh Mr. Mentor, I've so missed seeing your smiling face. Hawaii is where it all began. Do you know—"

George laughed, interrupting, "Hey, I don't even have my drink yet and you're starting."

Cherry pipe smoke spiraled above his head and scented the air around us. "But I have something important to tell you," I said. "When I asked you what kind of work I would do, you always said, 'talk'. You drove me crazy. I mean really crazy!" George's deep laugh started in his belly and moved up to his throat. As our drinks arrived he took a sip of his flaming concoction, licked his lips, and sat back.

"It's amazing that you're here in Hawaii at this exact time," I exclaimed. "I'm booked as the keynote presenter to a large conference of executives from around the world."

He sipped his drink and gave me a questioning look. "That's good. What are you going to talk about?"

"The plane crash and how to handle change. I've prepared, done my research, studied my notes and yet, it seems my message is almost too simple and unsophisticated. How can my story of surviving a plane crash inspire others? I'm afraid it's not important enough." No sooner had I said it than I realized I'd used the 'fear' word, afraid of being inadequate. I could already tell by George's silence that he was revving up to remedy my apprehension.

Puffing on his pipe, he reviewed, "Let's get back to basics. Why do you think they hired you?"

"I'm not really sure," I said evasively.

"Oh, yes you do. You overcame tremendous fear when you faced death in that accident. Everyone in the human race has fears. Doesn't matter how important they are, or how much money they have. What you're going to talk about is a real life experience. Tell them what you learned, what your priorities in life are, and how you overcame fear to take the witness stand to speak for the victims and improve safety regulations."

I watched him while thinking, how would my presentation come together?

George was mesmerized by the ash-laced orange-and-plum-colored sunset. Several seconds later he said, "You got steak from the plane crash and sizzle from the Hollywood years. When you speak, put some steak and sizzle into it and they'll listen. But even more importantly, don't forget to tell those people how they can change. Give them some insights into finding purpose and happiness."

"I know you're right and I get your point, but—and I mean but—it still sounds too simple, too hokey."

"It's not hokey at all; people are the same the world over. Humanity has the same hopes, loves, expectations, and doubts. Do you recall when I said you were born to talk? That's how you help people help themselves, through your speeches. It's what you claim for your destiny. It's what you manifest."

"I don't have a handle on what you mean. Manifest my speaking? How the heck do I do that?"

Deep in thought, he flared a match and re-lit his pipe. "I've got a little recipe I put together to help people understand what manifestation is. Once you understand it, you can put it into action and some darn good things can happen."

"You've got me going, Mr. Wise Sage, what's this intriguing recipe?"

He chuckled. "Okay, Partner. Let's say you really want something. You put the five A's to work for you."

"The five A's?"

"Those are the ingredients. Of course, you have to manifest them in the right order, kind of like baking a cake. Are you ready to listen?"

I rolled my eyes. "Of course."

He held up his index finger and said, "First, *acknowledge* what it is you want. Then, *accept* it as yours, like you already have it. Next, ease back a little and *ask if it is for your highest good*. Now, you take *action* to make it happen. Here's the good part. You may not have what you want yet, but you still give *appreciation* that the Universe is providing for you. Sometimes what you ask for happens right away and sometimes it takes awhile. Are you getting it?"

"I think so. Let's see if I understand this. You're telling me I can manifest the right thing to say to people. I'll know inside of me that what I'm saying is what they need to hear. Exactly how am I going to pull that one off?"

"Think about the speeches you've already given. Anything special happen?"

Smiling briefly, I recalled, "Yes. Sometimes after my presentation, a person from the audience stops me and says, 'You were talking directly to me.'"

"Good. When you look out in the audience and you speak the universal language of truth, you'll see understanding in their eyes." He gestured with his hand. "Not everyone is going to like everything you say. Don't let that put you in a tailspin. When people are ready to accept change, they will absorb the information."

"How can I be certain what I have to say is what people need to hear?" I questioned.

"You know when you know."

"You've been saying that to me for years, George."

"I can't make it any easier to understand than that."

"I have a headache thinking about tomorrow," I said while pressing a hand to my forehead.

"That's because you're prejudging yourself. Hone your skills, be prepared, and know that polish and perfection are only a part of your presentation. If you speak from your heart you'll help people find their path."

"Are you sure it's not too simplistic?"

"Yup."

"It is strange how life works. In first grade Mrs. Miller, my teacher—God rest her soul—said everyone could go to lunch except me because I was too dumb to read out loud. Aghh, that was painful. I was too petrified to speak up. My parents were divorcing and things were very unsettling at home. By the time I was in high school, I was still too afraid to try out for a school play. Unbelievable. Now I'm taking my greatest weakness and making it my best asset."

"I know it wasn't easy but that's what you need to do in this lifetime. Conquer your fears and push past them. Don't let them control you."

Hesitating, I said, "Easier said than done. I love speaking ... I'll give it my best shot."

"Now you're cooking; each time you speak you'll get a little better at it."

"Right." I wanted to believe him. I really did. "Maybe I should be drinking the volcano drink tonight instead of the fruit juice."

"You stay on the juice," he commented, his face crinkling up into a huge smile. "You have to give a speech tomorrow morning. By the way, where will it be held?"

"In the main ballroom at the Sheraton Hotel here in Waikiki at 8:00 AM."

"Good." He waved for the check and said, "We'd better call it a night. You need your rest. You'll do great tomorrow without a doubt; you love to talk."

By the time I returned to my hotel, my headache had disappeared. I read over my notes, made some minor changes, and went to bed. Waking at four in the morning with a case of the jitters, my brain was on overload.

Arriving at the hotel ballroom early in the morning, I felt overwhelmed by the size of the room. This was my largest audience ever. As people poured into the reception area to chat with one another over bagels and coffee, I was amazed at the attendance and my hands felt clammy. My intellectual mind was saying, *I can't do this.* Fighting back, my spiritual wisdom was saying, *I can do this.*

The emcee signaled me to stand behind the curtain. My anxiousness escalated as I waited through ten agonizing minutes of acknowledgements and introductions. I shook my arms to ease the stress, coughed, and swallowed several times to relieve tightness in my throat. When it finally came time to introduce me, the emcee announced:

"Let me first set the scene. It's March 1, 1978. Our speaker is on

Continental Flight 603 from Los Angeles to Honolulu to emcee the
Miss Hawaii Pageant. This day changed her life forever."

My insides plummeted as the room went dark and the plane crash
sound effects filled the air. I shuddered through each second of the
dramatic audio opening. Gasping for breath, I heard the questions:

Do you love yourself?
Do you have a good relationship
with your family and friends?
Are you living your goals and dreams?
If you die today, have you left this
planet a better place for being here?

The sound effects wound to a finish as my voice screamed, "I want
to live!" Walking to center stage, I announced, "I'm Donna Hartley.
I'm alive and loving life. I'm here this morning to ask you two
important questions: Are you really alive? Are you loving your life?"

The applause was spontaneous. I recited my next line as my
confidence was slowly building. I was moving into my comfort zone.
This is the moment I live for. I wasn't in the past; I wasn't in my
future; I was in the present. As I glimpsed the faces in the audience, I
saw him near the back of the room—the familiar face of George. He
raised his arms and clasped his hands together in a winning salute.
Then he turned and disappeared through the double doors.

Journal
Ride the Wave

Do what you love
and do it with passion
then it becomes your success

I'm sitting on the lanai beneath a waning crescent moon, writing about my new insights. Surfing put me back in touch with the ocean. Yes, my carefree college days in the islands. What would my life be like if I had stayed in Hawaii? I had dated a fair share of men and had marriage proposals with diamond rings, but why hadn't I accepted? Why ... why ... why ... It didn't feel right. I was destined for something else.

Dear George showed up unexpectedly and shared with me the five A's: **Acknowledge** what I want. **Accept** it as mine, like I already have it. Ease back and **ask if it is for the highest good**. Take **action** to make it happen. Show **appreciation** that the Universe is providing for me. Today, I stood on stage and must admit at first I was terrified. Let me see, is there another word stronger than terrified? Petrified is good. Once I began speaking, my concerns slowly disappeared. When the lights are on me I'm not worrying about my past or thinking about my future—I'm in the now. My speech was a success. Yeah, I did it. Isn't that what Catharina and Raimund tried to instill in me, to live in the moment?

I am THANKFUL! I'm thankful to be in Hawaii. I am thankful for Chuck. I am thankful for Dr. Bob. I'm thankful to surf. I'm thankful for George. I'm thankful to be a speaker.

Chapter Ten

Face Your Fears

You have to believe
you deserve a life of fulfillment

"Nothing Down Real Estate Seminar." *Hmmm, an interesting concept, or a typical huckster rip-off?* The brochure kept my attention as I read it from cover to cover. I quickly added up how much rent I had paid over the past twenty years and it was staggering. I wanted my own home, but my business swallowed up any profits I created. Checking my bank account, I saw that I had $400 extra, and the seminar was $399. I wrote the check and was off to Reno for the weekend course. All I could hear were my friends saying, "Now, you have no money to buy a house."

The real estate expert suggested looking for a seller who would entertain a "lease to buy" option instead of paying a large down payment. I could move in immediately and pay higher monthly payments, which would go toward the purchase price of the property. All the rent that I paid to the seller would go toward my down payment, and I could close eighteen months later.

It made sense to me, so why not. Every weekend I went house hunting and soon found one that I couldn't live without. It was cozy with beautiful blooming trees, oodles of windows, and a view of Lake Tahoe. The owner, Joanne, was going through a divorce and moving out of the area. It was all those little zeros at the end of the selling price that had me asking for divine guidance. In fact, it was $100,000 more than I expected to pay. The real issue was, nothing in my bank account. I did, however, have speeches booked, so there would be an income. Yes, I was counting on the future and I was feeling optimistic. It was time to see how this would play out.

I was so nervous yet so excited to make my first offer on a house. I'd move in, live in the house, pay double rent, and all that money would go toward the down payment. Even though it wasn't listed with possible owner financing, I thought it was a brilliant idea, but to my surprise the owner flatly refused the offer. "I know this is the house for me," I blurted out in an innocent tone to Joanne. "It's meant to be mine. No one else can buy it." In hindsight, I shouldn't have been that blunt. In fact, she likely thought I was a lunatic. Realizing I'd really bungled the offer, I suffered a sleepless night filled with tears.

The next morning, I made up my mind to stay optimistic and forge ahead. Returning to the house, I took pictures of the outside and tacked them up throughout my rental unit. I actually envisioned myself living there.

When the house hadn't sold by the following month, I felt ready to make another offer. Joanne didn't refuse the offer, but she didn't acknowledge it either. Still hopeful, I continued to visualize myself living in the house. Four weeks later, I made my third offer. Again, no answer. I was so sure she would acquiesce that I purchased a sofa, loveseat, and chair for the living room. How crazy is that? I even had to store the loveseat at a friend's house because it wouldn't fit in my rental house. **Action**—that's what I was creating.

As I made my fourth offer, I was convinced I'd get the key to

Donna Hartley

the front door. Silence from the other end sent me into a colossal depression. Joanne made it painfully clear she was not interested. Feeling vulnerable and powerless, I was ready to give up at last. Now I was sure I had misinterpreted my intuition. I drove past the house with the remnants of my resolve fading away like an ebbing tide.

A few days later, returning from a long hike that burned off some frustration, I heard the phone ring. George snickered as he spoke, "You know, Partner, I've never been to Lake Tahoe. How does next week sound?"

His timing was right on. "Great! How is it you always know when I need you? You are amazing! How do you do that?"

"You know when you know. Like I know it's time for me to come to Tahoe."

George's timing was uncanny. He knew when I was floundering and needed to see him face to face.

As I pulled up in the "arrivals" lane at the Reno-Tahoe airport the following Friday, George was waiting outside. I was ecstatic to see him. Though we talked on the phone on a regular basis, seeing him was a rare treat. His eyes crinkled with a big smile and he rubbed his hands together saying, "It sure is cold here. Feels like snow."

I dropped him off at the lodge where he had booked a room. The next morning when I picked him up, it was already blowing snow. He sauntered outside dressed for a blustery Tahoe day in jeans, western boots, a warm down jacket, and the familiar aroma of the tobacco from his blooming pipe.

The roads were slippery as I drove to the restaurant with more than a normal amount of caution. The pine trees, catching the snow in their branches, gave the appearance of a picture postcard. We found a table near a blazing fireplace and sat down. Scanning the menu, George said, "I'm having a big mountain breakfast and from the looks of you, a pancake or two would do you good. You need some strength if you're going to be stacking firewood for this winter."

As he finished polishing off his huge breakfast and was sipping a second cup of coffee, I broke the news.

I said dejectedly, "I've made four offers, all rejected. I've tried to stay positive, as you said I should, but haven't heard even a 'maybe' from the owner. I'm ready to quit."

George squinted and gave an insightful look. "Let's back up. Four offers you said. Why didn't the owner accept?"

"Because I made the offers with no money down. I was praying she would take a lease option."

George's face registered surprise. "Well, Partner, I don't think if I were her I'd take your terms either. I'd want some money down."

"Of course she'll get the money, but she won't get it all at once, because I have to go out and create it first. We've talked before about manifesting what you want. I actually imagined I was living there, and even bought new furniture. But now ... it won't happen." Staring into the fire, I felt deflated.

He sat back with a puzzled look on his face for a moment, then said, "Tell me about this lease option. Explain how it works."

As I filled in the details, he asked more questions while sipping his coffee.

"Is Joanne leaving the area?"

"She's already gone and has the house rented to tenants because it didn't sell."

"Why do you think she didn't accept your offer?" George probed.

"Because I think Joanne wanted the traditional deal. That is what she expected. She relocated out of the area and is renting a house in the foothills to see if she likes it there. She said she wants to take her time to be sure the community is right for her before she buys a home."

"Where there any other offers?" George questioned.

"Not that I am aware of. I took the seminar, did my homework, and followed through."

"Oh, so that's how you're looking at things. I meet with people from all over the world and, boy, do I hear excuses," he said, waving his hand to emphasize his point. "I failed at marriage, so why try again? I got fired, so now I'm washed up. I want to expand my business, but I'll never get a loan, so what's the use? The list goes on and on."

"Huh? What's that supposed to mean?"

"Stop buying into excuses and find a solution," George said pointedly.

"But I tried everything to stay positive."

George raised his eyebrows. "Wait a minute. You can't solve all your predicaments by covering up insecure feelings with just positive thoughts. Break new ground; find out what is limiting you. When you figure that out, you move beyond those barriers; that's a giant step toward your goal. Let yourself be powerful. Get in there and fight for what you want." He grinned and threw up his hands. "I'm off my soap box now."

"I thought that's what I was doing." I paused for a moment to review. "On the outside I'm following through by making offers but what's limiting me is that I don't believe I deserve this house. How can I be sure I can afford it?"

"It's simple; you have to do the work first. How did you ask for it?"

"George, I already told you all that," I moaned in exasperation.

"What I mean, Partner, is whether you ask for it every night?"

Slumping I replied, "Every day, and night too."

"Do you ask if it's for your highest good?"

"My highest good? I guess so; I thought I did. The house has an ideal layout—even a suite over the garage for my office."

"This house will give you roots and encourage you to work hard," he said. "There's always plenty to do and fix when you own a home. Why don't you show it to me?" He rose and smiled. "Whoever thought you'd be Susie Homemaker?"

In the car, I turned to face him. "There are tenants in the house. We can't get in."

"We'll pull in the driveway and take a look. You're going to be the new owner, right?"

As we drove down the street, I noticed George looking off to the left side of the road. "Stop the car," he said, and pointed his index finger. "That house over there, now that fits you. I like it. The pine trees and all the windows in the front; you can see the mountains."

"That's it! That's the house."

"Pull in the driveway."

"What? There are renters."

"Do you want this house?" George commandingly queried.

I mutely nodded. He pointed, and I pulled in the driveway.

He scrutinized the house with a perceptive look on his face, asking, "Have you done everything possible to own this house?"

"Yes." I reviewed the list of all the things I had done.

"Do you see yourself in it every day?"

"Well, I used to. Not anymore," I pouted.

George turned to me and asked, "Have you ever watched a marathon race?"

"Sure, why do you ask?"

"Humor me. Tell me about it."

"Okay. They start running and eventually the leaders come out of the pack and move ahead of the rest. Humored?"

George snorted and asked, "Do they all stay out in front?"

"No. Some get cramps and quit and others lose their energy."

"Now we're getting somewhere. What about those in the back of the pack? Ever seen the ones who keep pumping along real steady and focused? Did you ever see one of them pull out of the pack, move out in front, and win the race?"

I nodded. "I've seen that."

"How do you suppose they did it?"

"Train hard and mentally never lose sight of their goal?"

George suddenly smiled. "You've got it. Winners never waver in their belief in themselves and they never give up. Now stop letting your fears prevent you from owning this house. Remember, it is not the seller who is stopping the sale ... it's you."

Renewed confidence was slowly taking root. "I'm getting the picture. I guess I needed some coaching, Mr. Miracle Worker."

"That's better. When you're alone tonight, ask if this house is for your highest good. If the answer you feel is yes, get hopping and make another offer. Now, how about taking me on a little tour of the lake?"

"Sure," I giggled. "While I drive, you think about what you're going to buy me for a housewarming gift. Make it a nice one."

 Journal
Face Your Fears

The more powerful your vision
the more it demands of you

Home ... a home. I'm like anyone else. I dream about having my own place. I want to hang pictures, paint the walls the colors I like, and create a garden in the backyard.

Single and buying a home is crazy scary. First, can I afford it? No. Second, if things go wrong, can I fix them? No. So here I am in my same pattern of doubt, but can I legitimately say that I deserve and will earn the money?

Just when I need him, George appears. I wonder if he has hidden angel wings?

After a lumberjack's breakfast he gave me the lecture of a lifetime. Summing it up, he demanded I find out what my limiting beliefs were and break those barriers. He nailed it; I must determine the highest good. He used one of his Georgeisms to make me discover the answer to my own dilemma. His Georgeisms drive me nuts.

Become aware of your limiting beliefs
It is your right to change them

I believe if the house is for my highest good, it's mine. The amazing thing is George even called me Susie Homemaker. I am so thrilled he came to Tahoe. I wonder if I'll ever understand how he knows to show up at the right time. He's clairvoyant. I need to make another offer, follow my heart, and live my dream. Will she or won't she accept it?

Chapter Eleven

Action Creates Attraction

Road blocks happen
Be persistent to fulfill your dreams

Watching the pure white snow flutter from the sky, I was fortifying my resolve to make another offer on the house. A month had passed since George's visit to Tahoe and each day, night, and in-between I repeated, *If the house is for my highest good, I will have it.* Had I done everything I could? Had I conquered my limiting beliefs? Had I confirmed that I could and would earn it? Yes, yes, yes. I did deserve this home with a front lawn surrounded by Douglas fir and aspen trees and a stone fireplace in the quaint living room.

My hand trembled as I wrote another lease option offer to Joanne, the owner of my dream house. I would pay double rent for eighteen months and it would apply toward my down payment. I mailed my final offer after hugging the envelope for ten minutes. Figuring the mail delivery time, she should have the offer in two days. I waited and I waited. Nothing, *nada*. Mid-January, late January, early February, mid-February.

Then, while getting dressed for work, the phone rang. Joanne, my resistant seller, said, "Happy Valentine's Day to the most persistent person I have ever met. I'm accepting your offer."

Elated, speechless, I wondered what had changed her mind. Was it, as George insisted, my energy that had to change? Once I believed I was worthy of the house, it was mine. In hindsight, this principle seemed simple enough but was difficult to live.

"Joanne, this is the best Valentine's present I could ever ask for. You won't regret it."

She replied, "I know you'll love the house. I'll have the paperwork sent over within the week."

My mind was already churning out ways to create the money I'd need for the payments. I didn't get flowers or candy on Valentine's Day; I got my highest good instead.

I thanked her wholeheartedly, hung up, and dialed a familiar number. "Come on, pick up!"

"Hey Partner," George said. "Getting enough snow up there?"

"You bet, but this year, I can't wait for spring."

"Something going on with you, Donna? What about skiing?"

"I got a Valentine's present, George. A big, big present." It warmed my heart to hear him chuckle, knowing he'd been right all along.

"Patience and persistence. The man upstairs never gets tired of surprising the deserving. Pretty amazing, huh? When do you move in?"

"Not until summer. I don't know how I can wait, but it'll take that long to figure out how to make the payments."

"I believe in you. You believe in you and you'll do it."

I laughed. "Oh yeah, that's what I needed to hear. Now, start thinking about that housewarming gift."

I worked all the time and late into the evenings, calling clients, giving speeches, conducting trainings, and saving money. I searched the newspapers for bargains and was first at garage sales. Finally the day arrived, and as I couldn't afford a moving van, I lugged boxes, hoisted mattresses, and carted furniture.

Imagine owning my own home. I was so keyed up I couldn't sleep, getting out of bed in the middle of the night to walk from room to room. Overcome with emotion, tears of joy would well up in my eyes and I would glance at the ceiling, quietly saying, "Thank you."

Renting out my "office studio" over the garage gave me some extra income. I could use my dining room as a temporary office, a practical idea since I couldn't afford to eat right now. I hung café curtains in the bedrooms and bought warm comforters for the beds. My new sofa, loveseat, and chair were an ideal fit for the living room. A fresh coat of paint created a nice contrast to the warm redwood trim. My dining room featured an expansive patio door, and the view was bursting with life. Buds sprouted, flowers bloomed, and picturesque pine trees circled protectively. The indoor focal point was my cherished collection of framed photographs residing on the mantle over the stone hearth. As a reminder of how far I'd come, I placed a picture of the plane crash in the very center.

First a house; next a family. Not to rush it, I would start with a pet, a little warm-blooded companion to love. As a child I had fluffy Chow dogs, birds, rabbits, chickens, and even a duck named Quacky. Due to my work schedule and overnight travel I felt the best pet for me would be a cat. I wanted something soft to cuddle, so every night before I went to sleep, I asked, *How do I find the right cat for me?*

In the early hours of morning, between sleep and wakefulness, she came to me. She was definitely fluffy and white, with captivating blue eyes. She had the grey markings of a Himalayan on her face and tail. I climbed out of bed and paced the house, talking to myself, repeating the name I had heard. "Sheba ... Sheba ... Sheba ..." I chuckled. Just the name sounded spoiled.

The next day I scoured the newspaper ads, looking for Himalayan cats. Making some appointments, I started my search. At the first place, the mother cat snarled and the kittens ran away. At the next house, the kittens were adorable but ignored me. The last house I came to was in Grass Valley, and belonged to a tiny elderly lady who bred Himalayans as a hobby. Her name was Kitty. That was odd; my mother's nickname was Kitty. What really astounded me was that she had a daughter named Donna. Strange, I thought, or was it a sign?

Kitty, the nurturing grandmother type, loved her kittens. She had five litters for me to choose from. How would I find my Sheba with so many little fluffy things running around pawing, mewing, and chasing their tails? While sitting on the floor playing with the adorable balls of fur, I pondered how to make the right decision. After awhile the kittens became bored and went to play elsewhere, except for one. This determined little female tried to crawl up my leg and kept falling off. Finally, I set her on my lap and was admiring how beautiful she was with her grey markings, when she jumped off, right into my purse, where she sat staring at me with her big blue eyes. At that instant I knew she was my cat Sheba!

Kitty shook her head. "She's the pick of the litter, the most expensive." I talked Kitty into taking installments, and my cute high-priced cat had a new mom and a new home. The first week home she meowed all night because she wasn't able to jump up on my bed, so I gave in and hoisted her up. She picked my only down pillow as her own and settled into a contented sleep. Sheba became my constant companion, her little feet scurrying to keep up with me. Even in the backyard my Queen Sheba was right next to me, digging in the garden with her tiny little paws, looking like a dirt devil. She loved to step on daisies, move back, and watch them pop up, doing this over and over again, simply mesmerized. If only humans were so easily amused.

Speaking, traveling, stacking wood, and preparing my home for the cold winter months were rewarding times. Sheba was maturing into an exquisite cat who was also my sounding board, listening to every one of my new ideas. Late one evening during the first snowfall of winter, I lit a roaring fire and she curled up beside me. My journal was on my lap as I gazed at the snow-covered pine trees and reflected on the reasons for my contentment. I had a career, a house, and a cat. I didn't have the whole package yet, but at least I had begun to carve out a life for myself. What would happen next? For a quick second I had an unsettled feeling.

Journal
Action Creates Attraction

Don't give up

Buying the house wasn't easy. All right, that is an understatement but with George's help, I overcame my major stumbling blocks. Visualizing is the key—then add in patience, persistence, and work. I thought I would never get this house. Took me over a year!

My home gives me a feeling of security. I love having roots. Yeah, I have a yard. These Sierra Mountains are powerful and I gain strength from them. This is the best place for me to live. Oh no, I am a mountain gal.

My cuddly little Sheba has brought much joy and lots of laughter. Boy, does she have energy. We are inseparable except when I have to travel. As soon as I begin to pack my suitcase, she hops inside and nestles against my clothing. Even though she can't travel with me, her fur always does! I adore her. She is a love ball.

Thank you for answered prayers, the house of my dreams, the passion I have for my career, and an affectionate cat who made my house a home. What is next on the journey?

Part III
The Dream

Chapter Twelve

Trust Your Intuition

Intuition is powerful

Thanksgiving weather in the mountains was as unpredictable as winning the lottery. On this chilly "turkey day" the temperature was in the low thirties and the wind off the lake was blustery. The last vestiges of the aspen and maple leaves frolicked in my headlights as I drove through my quaint town of Tahoe City. I had nowhere to go but home for Thanksgiving dinner, which would be a chicken breast rather than the traditional turkey feast. I recalled the years before when I had been surrounded by many friends and even a boyfriend. But since being on this spiritual quest, life had changed. I resigned myself to go home alone, light a fire, and feed the cat.

Suddenly, a grinding thump from beneath my four-wheel drive warned me that something was drastically wrong. The steering wheel stubbornly resisted my attempt to turn, but I managed to maneuver the car to the side of the road. As I sat helpless, wondering what to do, a kind soul pulled up in a Jeep and offered to call a tow truck. Thanking her, I sat back to wait.

After the tow truck arrived and the driver was hitching my car to the back, I noticed another car pull up behind us. A handsome man got out and I knew him as the owner of a local business. I'd had a brief conversation with him once, but didn't know him well.

He walked over to where I stood shivering in my light jacket and said, "Looks like you have a problem. Can I help? Do you need a ride?"

It wasn't unusual for a local to offer assistance, and with the snow flurries and the bitter blowing wind, I would really appreciate a ride. Smiling up at him, I realized I had never paid attention to how tall and good-looking he was. I glanced back at the tow truck driver struggling with the hitch and said, "You know, that sounds great. I live a few miles down the road and I'm freezing."

"I'm going that way myself. No problem." He stuck out his hand. "By the way, my name is Matt."

Shaking his hand, I said, "I'm Donna. Glad you came along."

During the small talk on the drive home, I got around to asking him, "Why aren't you with friends or family, feasting on all the Thanksgiving goodies tonight?"

"Actually, I was invited, but didn't want to be the odd man out with no date. How about you?" Matt questioned.

I laughed. "Me too. I mean, I don't have a date either."

He hesitated, and then asked, "How about we have dinner next week?"

"Sure, I'll give you my number."

After he dropped me off, I warmed my hands by the fire and smiled when I recalled how his eyes revealed more than a flicker of interest. The night wasn't a total disappointment after all; I had met someone nice and attractive.

That evening was the beginning of a fun-loving relationship with Matt. We searched out wonderful restaurants and saw the latest movies. Month after delightful month our active schedule included snow-skiing, hiking, tennis, boating, and even bodysurfing in Hawaii.

Having finished another speaking engagement in the islands, Matt and I were lying on a Hawaiian beach watching the waves roll in and enjoying the refreshing ocean breeze. He said, "This is my kind of life. I want to stay here forever. I don't ever want to go back to work."

I poked him playfully. "Dream on. We've been in Hawaii seven days. I love it here too, but we have to go home tomorrow."

He pouted all that night like a child. The next morning while we were boarding the plane, he complained again about not wanting to leave Hawaii.

Back in Tahoe we got busy in our routines. I was shocked at how fast a year went by, then two, and then three, and time keep moving on as we would be nearing another year. It seemed to me we had so much in common and I felt my prayers had been answered. I thought marriage must be on the horizon. However, when I mentioned the "commitment" word to Matt, he'd say, "Heck, we're having a good time right now. You're such a great travel partner, Donna, and a superb skier. Aren't you having fun? Let's not spoil it."

One day, while at the park adjacent to the lake, I was watching children play. I gazed at Matt's tan face, saying, "I want a family, honey. That's so important to me."

He swiveled his head and uttered, "Unbelievable! Did you see that?"

"What?"

"The boat that barreled by. It's a classic."

After dinner that night, I was paging through a magazine and held it up to display a picture of a beautiful baby girl. "Look at this," I exclaimed. "Isn't she adorable? I want a daughter."

"Yeah, yeah. Hey, hand me the *TV Guide*," Matt said. "There's this great action movie and I think it's on tonight."

It took several more times, but I eventually picked up on the pattern. Whenever I would mention a family, Matt would immediately change the subject. I figured I should concentrate on getting married first and worry about the family later. Good idea; don't put the cart before the horse.

Matt moved in and his name went on the paperwork for the ownership of the house. Now I thought we could get married. Only problem was, his non-committal behavior persisted. Every so often I would gently bring up the subject of our relationship. "How about a small wedding in Hawaii?" In the back of my mind I was afraid my time clock was running out, and I'd soon be too old to have a child.

He continued to deflect my commitment questions with another question like, "Should we eat in, or out?" "There's a new movie in town, do you want to go tonight?" "Let's go skiing—there's fresh powder."

I assumed most couples had this problem before committing. Where was the reassurance of an engagement ring, marriage, and the promise of having a family?

More months passed and Matt and I kept busy planning our "to do" list. I loved motivational speaking with a passion. Yet, when I talked about work, Matt became cranky and disinterested. He made no secret of hating his work.

I would say, "As much as I love my career, it's sad you don't even talk about yours."

His response was, "Then you should work more because you like it. I don't want to work anymore. Hawaii sounds great to me."

He would come around in time. How could he not? I was doing everything to make him happy. But in truth, our relationship was beginning to slide and I felt it was my responsibility to hold us together. Finally, one evening as we sat in the dim light of a warm fire, I summoned up the courage to say, "Look, when are we going to get married?"

The room was silent except for the flames popping in the fireplace. Reluctantly, he said, "Donna, I don't have the money right now. I can't afford to buy you a ring. I know you want a beautiful diamond."

I could have danced on air. "Is that all that's stopping you?"

He nodded.

Before I fell to sleep, I had myself convinced the only thing keeping Matt from marrying me was a diamond ring. A very solvable problem, but deep—and I mean deep—in my heart, I knew our relationship was struggling.

Over the next few weeks, Matt became more withdrawn. I found myself spending more time with Sheba than with him. Frequent walks were my salvation. On my walks I would ask the question, would I marry Matt? The answer my intuition was screaming at me was "No." I'd say to myself, *Tomorrow I'll ask the question again,* thinking the answer would be different.

When I repeatedly told Matt how much I loved him and wanted to spend my life with him, he would smile, nod, and change the subject. Finally, to shut me up, Matt agreed to marry me, but only if I would be the breadwinner. In my mind, I rationalized that was manageable; yes, work harder and make more money.

After speaking in Los Angeles I purchased a beautiful diamond and sapphire ring to solve the ring problem. My girlfriend Brooke, who had spent a week hiking and sweating with me at the Ashram, was with me. She loved the ring but only shook her head, asking, "Donna, do you know what you're doing?"

After I'd returned home I held out my sparkling left hand, announcing, "Hey, Mr. Bridegroom, look at this. I even bought a simple white dress, perfect for a Hawaiian wedding."

His response was, "I don't want to talk about it right now," and he walked away.

Following him like a little puppy dog into the living room I asked, "Why? Is business bad?"

"Yes."

I paused to digest what he'd said and dropped the subject, but I wasn't going to let him off that easily. The next weekend Matt said he needed time to think and was going away alone. My disappointment was evident.

After he returned, he remained distant. I figured the reason was his wallet, which was decidedly empty. Desperate by now, I became even more obsessed with having a wedding date.

"Talk to me," I begged. "Let's have dinner together and work this out." I knew I was overcompensating, but I convinced myself that everyone in a relationship had to compromise.

When he went off alone again for two more weekends, I knew something was definitely wrong. My denial lasted until one afternoon when Matt was out skiing. Call it destiny, or whatever, but the volume was turned up on his answering machine and I overheard a message from a woman saying, "I miss you, Matt. I can hardly wait till I see you. I'm so excited about this weekend in Carmel. The weather will be wonderful for bike riding."

My heart plummeted, setting my mind awhirl. Feeling lightheaded, I sank down on a chair, unable to accept what I'd heard. How could this be? I played the message again and again until I had no choice but to believe Matt was involved with another woman. I resisted a hysterical scream as I gasped for air.

Half an hour later, his car pulled in the driveway and I quickly decided how to handle the situation. Taking several deep breaths, I composed myself. Then, walking outside I said, "Missed you today. How was skiing?"

Matt was unloading his skis with his back to me. "Actually, it was great."

His words turned me inside out. A sudden boldness surged through me and I said, "It's been awhile since we've been away. Let's plan something special for this weekend."

He turned, and then frowned, formulating a response. After a brief smile he said, "I've already decided to spend this weekend on the coast."

I clenched my fists in anger and struggled to keep from screaming. "Oh, that sounds like the place for us to go. I haven't been to the coast in a long time."

"Well, I only made arrangements for me," Matt said tersely. "You said you were working."

"I've changed my mind. Let's go for it." I swallowed hard and continued, "We can go for a bike ride."

"I can't get reservations this late. You don't want to stay in some dump."

I pushed on. "Let's go for it. We'll find something."

"I don't have any extra money, Donna. I can't afford some fancy hotel for the two of us."

The tension between us was supercharged. "I'll pay."

I had decided to give Matt time to be honest. I needed to hear what he would say. My inner thoughts were pleading, *Please Matt, be honest. Tell me the truth. We can work this out.*

He shook his head, and with a sour look said, "No."

I exploded, "Your phone rang. I heard the message! What is her name?" His eyes widened for an instant, but he didn't utter a sound. "If you meet with her this weekend our relationship is over," I screamed. He still said nothing. "Say something!" I yelled. Matt turned and stormed into the house.

By the next morning, the thought of him leaving to be with another woman had me feeling sick inside. I became desperate and stooped to an all-time low, begging him not to leave me.

"I'm going," he said flatly. He packed his clothes and walked out the door. Becoming hysterical, I rolled into a little ball, rocked back and forth, and cried. My opportunity to have a child before I was too old had gone out the door with him.

I was furious at myself. I had taken dozens of walks and always asked the question, would he marry me? I didn't listen to my intuition because my inner voice told me, *No he's not going to marry you.* I had manipulated our relationship, convincing myself I could make it work. Had I ever once asked if he was for my highest good?

The next three days were emotional bedlam. When Matt returned, he acted as if nothing had happened and resumed his lifestyle of choice. The next weekend, when he disappeared again, I said nothing. In such a diminished state, I didn't know what to do. I was so embarrassed I didn't want to discuss what was happening to me with anyone—not George or even my close girlfriends. However, when he came back, I summoned up the courage and insisted we talk. Matt's response was to get off the sofa, go into the bedroom, lock the door and turn on the TV.

By now, the chilling dread that I had made a colossal mistake by putting his name on the ownership to the house had turned into hellish reality. What I feared the most happened.

"You have to move out; this is not working."

He answered in a chilling voice, "I own half of this house. I live here. I'm not moving."

Smoldering with anger, I managed to maintain my composure but in the following days the stress was unbearable. We treated one another like strangers. I couldn't sleep, lost weight, and my work suffered. The anxiety was making me ill with the two of us living together in a hostile environment. In a candid moment I said, "I want you and your affair out of here, Matt. I can't live with you in the same house."

"My condo is rented. I can't kick the tenants out."

After more attempts to make him leave I consulted an attorney. My lawyer met with Matt, and after lengthy negotiations he said to me, "This is not a first-rate guy; pay him off and get on with your life." I was shocked at the exorbitant amount of money I had to pay Matt to get him out of the house and off the deed. I had to write him a $5,000 check that day to have him pack his bags. My monthly payments to him would continue for the next three years and then the house would revert back to me. My attorney convinced me it was the only way.

In his lawyer tone he said, "This guy will not negotiate. You'll spend years in court and lots of money fighting him. An even worse scenario: what if you had married him? He would have cheated on you."

Taking my lawyer's advice, I resigned myself to paying. A painful lesson; hell yes!

Matt moved out and then I learned his girlfriend was much younger. I'd crossed over the forty mark and she was still in her twenties. The next insult was that he moved her into his condo. We lived in such a small town; I'd see them together constantly, holding hands. I was financially strapped, paying the mortgage and the monthly installments to Matt. My worst anxiety was whether I could make enough money or would I lose the house to him. His parting words were, "You can't do it. I'll get the house."

He was right, I couldn't afford it all, but his vindictive words ignited my determination to prove him wrong.

Journal
Trust Your Intuition

Intuition is powerful

My commitment is to release denial and to trust my gut feelings. How could I have been so stupid as to sacrifice my self-worth for the sake of a man? I wasted four years of my life with a guy who didn't love me. The signs were all there: his lack of communication and non-committal attitude, his disinterest in family and children. My intuition was screaming that Matt would not marry me but I was too stubborn to listen. I thought I could change him. Matt was not right for me, but I forced the relationship because I wanted my dream of having a husband and a child to come true.

George has been adamant for years that first I must love myself before anyone else would love me. Why do I repeat this self-defeating pattern? Why is this ingrained in me? How do I change this? I thought I was loving and accepting myself but I'm not there yet!

Thank you Universe for this tough lesson, and I claim it. My neediness was a major part of the problem. I accept this lesson and vow to never repeat it. Let me restate this, I get it. I VOW TO HONOR MYSELF.

Chapter Thirteen

Pay More Attention

What you don't know about yourself
controls you

My eyes blinked open ... each one felt like a pound of sand was in it. Slowly, I raised my head off the pillow. The muscles in my body ached. Cautiously, my fingers felt my puffy face and the bags under my eyes. My bed appeared like a tornado had passed through; an indication of another restless night.

Upon waking, the first emotion I felt was rage. I was furious at my ex-boyfriend. I felt used, tired—a has-been, cast away for another woman—in fact, a younger woman. A guttural scream erupted from my throat. "Never, never, never will I allow a man to use me." Tears welled up in my eyes.

The next emotion that enveloped me was disdain for myself. I had been so needy. I was blind-sided by my own ego. Since the breakup with Matt, my emotional chaos kept me in hell, bouncing back and forth from rage to depression. I had to do something. Something so I wouldn't go insane.

I started up the steps to my office. I felt like I was sinking in quicksand, but continued up the staircase. It was time to focus my attention on my business and leave the pity party behind. Fortunately, I had hired a marketing director, Jeanette, several months back. While I was trying to build a life with Matt, she was looking after the business, calling clients and booking speeches. She was dependable, knowledgeable, and had loads of confidence. My calendar was filling up with bookings. A couple of years younger than me, Jeanette dressed with style and good fashion sense. Her trademark was the huge designer tote bag she carried with her everywhere.

It was time for me to create some financial abundance. I was determined not to let Matt have the house. I needed two dozen more speaking engagements. How would I fire up my audiences if I couldn't even fire up myself? Discussing the situation with Jeanette, she was comforting, understanding, and a much-needed shoulder to cry on.

It all started to unravel the next day when I couldn't find an important file; I thought my mind was playing tricks on me. Searching everywhere for it, I asked Jeanette, "Have you seen it?"

She smiled, shook her head, and said, "No. Don't worry. It will turn up. You've been under so much stress lately, you probably misplaced it."

I nodded, feeling my insides shift a little. Could I be that forgetful? "You know, maybe you're right because I can't find my travel alarm clock either."

"You probably forgot it at the last hotel where you stayed. Why don't you give them a call? Stress can play weird games with your memory, Donna."

"Humm. I suppose that's why I can't find my briefcase either. It's kind of scary, Jeanette ... to think I might be losing it."

She gave me a sympathetic smile. "No man is worth all the anguish you're going through. You get yourself better and let me worry about the business."

Her words were reassuring, but I needed to get back into the day-to-day routine of running the office—resume my responsibilities. Throwing myself into work would boost my shaky morale. I said, "I'm ready to sit down and go over the financials and the pending contracts. When can you make time?"

Jeanette looked dismayed. "I'm sorry, Donna. You know how busy I've been on the phone. I haven't had time to get all that together yet, but I'll have it for you soon. Don't worry. Just relax."

Stating sharply, "I am relaxed, Jeanette, I need to review my books," I could tell I had upset her. "Look," I said in a more congenial tone, "why don't I get on the phone and personally call some of the clients you have lined up. I always make it a point to talk with the contact person before I do my presentation."

"There's plenty of time for that, Donna. I'm trying to close two big contracts and don't want to lose them. It's a beautiful day; why don't you take a walk while I close these agreements. We'll talk later."

Walk, I didn't want to walk. I needed to work. An uneasy feeling crept into my stomach. An apprehensive sensation suggested something was wrong. I was still off balance from my breakup with Matt, so it must be me.

The next morning I was in the office and opened the petty cash envelope to take money out for postage. "Jeanette, there is no money." I questioned, "What happened to all the petty cash? I put a hundred dollars in here."

She shrugged, suggesting, "Maybe you used it all."

I tried to remember, but that only got me flustered. I pushed the subject from my mind. "Okay, okay. How about I call some of the clients you booked?"

"I have to finish up what's on my desk and then I'll get the files together." Jeanette smiled and cocked her head in thought. "Didn't you say you had to work on some new material for your speech? Why don't you do that first? I'll make a few more calls."

I'd been putting off refining certain parts of my presentation and doing it now made sense. When Jeanette finished making her calls, we could review the bookings together. I was well into my presentation when I overheard her make a few incorrect statements. As soon as she got off the phone I said, "Jeanette, you're misrepresenting me. I don't speak on negotiation skills."

She raised her hands in a gesture of reassurance. "You can speak on anything. Once we get the contract, we'll work through it."

"No," I insisted, "I do not speak on that topic."

Pointing her finger at me, Jeanette said, "I'm the marketing director and I'll handle this. Isn't that why you hired me?" She stared at me with a forced smile.

My mind reeling from her words, I walked out of the office to calm myself and think. Something was telling me there was a big problem, but was it her or me?

The next day, the stapler disappeared. I brushed it off as being misplaced. When I commented to Jeanette that I was missing one of my training manuals, she merely said, "It'll turn up." I mentioned that with the schedule so booked, the phones were exceptionally quiet. She insisted she'd kept in constant touch with the clients and there was no need for them to call.

On Friday, I received a large check for an upcoming speaking engagement. I had booked the contract but Jeanette had handled the details, so she would earn a large commission. For the first time since I hired her, Jeanette didn't come to work. Her boyfriend phoned to inform me she was ill and asked if he could come by to pick up her commission check.

On Monday, no Jeanette, and no phone call. I rang her home, and when I heard a message that the line was disconnected, a sharp chill ran through me. Frantically, I called the other numbers she had given me. Dead ends. I sat at my desk fighting back the rising tide of panic. Slowly, the grave enormity of my situation settled in. Jeanette was gone. My head was spinning and I hadn't a clue what state my business was in.

The next few days I studied the records. Nothing made sense. When I noticed conflicting dates, I began calling the clients. That's when I discovered the numbers were phony. At first I didn't want to believe it, and then I panicked. That was the beginning. The bookings slated were fictitious, and there were discrepancies in the office accounts.

After a few days of disbelief, I spoke with a friend on the police force who suggested I hire a private detective. After some research, the detective found where Jeanette was living. The investigation led to a search of her house that turned up over one hundred and twenty items stolen from my business and home. She had packed more in her tote bag than her lunch.

When it was all over, I had less than two hundred dollars to my name and only one authentic speaking engagement. I stood at my office window and stared at the lake. Hot tears burned in my eyes. Would I lose my home? Everything I had work so hard for? I prayed for a miracle.

I stayed in bed for the next three days, lifeless and sobbing until the tears ran out. It was ten years since the plane crash. I was asking "pity me" questions like: *Why was I betrayed by the two people I trusted most? Why did this happen to me? What did I do to deserve it?*

Late on the third day Sheba, my white fluffy ball of fur, climbed onto my bed and curled up on my chest. She lay there purring. When I looked into her eyes I saw, *Mom, I love you and need you.* Her comforting presence was soothing. She also seemed to say, *Get going Mom. I love this house and I ain't moving.*

In a dream-like state I had a premonition that George was reaching out to me, insisting that everyone has challenges in their life.

Pick yourself up
and get going
life is a series
of learning lessons

The next afternoon it was time to see Mel, my accountant, and ask his advice. He listened to my story, looked through my accounts, and calculated some numbers.

"Well Donna, here are the hard facts. Unless you have a hundred percent increase in your business within the next three months, you'll not only lose your company, but you'll lose your house as well."

"A hundred percent. How can I do that?" I wailed.

"Donna, you teach this stuff. Now is when you get to see if it really works. You can't blame the boyfriend and you can't blame the marketing director. They're long gone," he said. "You have to get to work, now. You built your business from nothing once before and you can do it again."

I sighed. "I don't have anything left. I feel ..."

"You feel what?" Mel asked gently.

I bowed my head and said, "I feel like a fool."

"Don't be so hard on yourself. You've accomplished more than most. I'm willing to bet you'll get through this."

I left Mel's office feeling even more depressed and decided to head straight for the Reno-Tahoe airport across the street. I checked on flights going to Denver and discovered the fare was lower than ever. I trusted my gut feeling. I wondered if there was enough room on my credit card and was thrilled to find out the charge went through. The flight was booked for the following weekend. I knew George was in Denver working for this month and I had to see him. My next mission was to call him.

His cheery greeting was, "Hi, Partner. Where have you been keeping yourself?"

Silent for a moment, I started to slowly admit the sad truth. "George, the reason I haven't called is because I didn't want you to know what was going on with me."

"That sounds pretty serious."

"I've been such a fool," I blurted out. "I've made terrible mistakes. I was on top of the world and got complacent and now I'm at risk of losing everything. I'm flying in late next Saturday afternoon. Can we go to dinner Saturday night? Please, I need your help. You said if I ever ..."

George heard the urgency in my voice. "Hang in there. My time is yours, Partner. Meanwhile, you take it easy. Don't do anything rash. You're not thinking of hurting yourself, are you?" he cautioned.

"Well ... no."

"Okay, then go hug your cat. I have a meeting, but call again if you need to talk and we will iron out the details. Come to Denver." He paused, and then in a serious tone he continued, "It's time. I have something important to tell you."

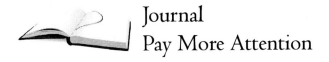

Journal
Pay More Attention

It's the choices
that make us who we are

Now that I am a little older and wiser—oh yes, and have some grey hairs too—I realize that life is full of peaks and valleys. Hadn't George told me dozens of times that life goes up and down and with every turn of fate comes a lesson? Don't look at it as good or bad, but understand what you need to learn from the experience. I comprehend what he tells me rationally but in reality I'm too stubborn. I'm a redhead, Irish, female, and Native American too. I didn't want to see what was going on. What did my marketing director teach me? She taught me that I was out of touch with my business. I didn't think I was good at marketing so I let someone else do it. I'LL PAY ATTENTION to every aspect of my life. If I was watching this episode on television I would say, "I can't believe she didn't see it coming! What a fool she is." It's pretty clear when you stand back and look at the total picture. I surely didn't see it coming because I wasn't paying attention.

Universe, I have learned that when you don't trust your instincts the lessons get harder. I promise right now to pay attention, and I mean a lot more attention. I'm thankful for my health, my house, and my cat who loves me. Please grant me the strength to pick up the pieces and put my life back together again one more time. This is getting old.

I'm closing with a Georgeism. *Life is simple; it's man who complicates it. Paraphrasing it in my terms, life is simple; it's me who complicates it.*

Chapter Fourteen

Learn Your Lessons

Your fears control you
until you confront them

The lady behind me curtly requested, "Could you please move? I want to get to my seat." Her words startled me. I moved down the aisle until I found my row. Tightening my seat belt, I knew I should be over my jittery nerves, but when I was entombed by metal my emotions surfaced. The plane accelerated, and my thoughts flashed to the crash ... the flames ... the smoke ... the people burning. _Quick, distract yourself,_ I thought. _Think happy thoughts about ... home! Oops, no, can't go there until you buy it back from the ex-boyfriend. Umm, so ... business! Nope, don't go there until you can recover from the embezzling employee. Okay ... work itself! You love to successfully speak and inspire others. Oh yeah, you have exactly one lonely booking._ My throat closed and I felt I couldn't breathe. Vigorously I massaged my neck. My rational mind was spinning out of control. _Stop ... stop ... get a grip ..._ My thoughts were disconnected. Could I hold on until I saw George? Would he be able to decipher this mess I got myself into?

Landing at the Denver airport, I called George immediately and took the shuttle to his favorite Mexican restaurant. The sun was brilliant, but the chill of my mood clouded over anything warm. I spotted him sitting at a table beneath a brightly striped umbrella, puffing away on his pipe.

"Hi, Partner!" He waved me over and gave me an affectionate hug. My heart came to life, hoping he would perform yet another miracle and help me understand how to escape my turmoil again.

After we sat down, George patiently waited for me to start. Heaving a deep sigh, I began, "I'm so ashamed I didn't listen to my gut feeling about what was going on around me, and now my life is in shambles. My boyfriend left me for a younger woman and my marketing director defrauded me, stole, and embezzled. I don't understand it; I truly believed things would continue to improve after the plane accident, and for a while, they did. I'm on a spiritual path working hard to clean up my thinking and actions. I can't describe the feeling, George, but I don't think I ..." Tears flooded my eyes.

"Hold on, Donna. You're not thinking about doing anything to harm yourself like you did when you were living in Los Angeles, are you?"

I stared at him. "Well," I admitted after a long pause, "I'd like to move to Montana and become a hermit. I'm so disappointed. The people I loved and trusted deceived me."

"So, you want to run away?" George sat puffing on his pipe, and then finally said, "Well, you can't spend the rest of your life as a hermit. Have you already forgotten what life is all about? It's about learning from your mistakes and picking yourself up when you fall down."

Muttering, he said, "Besides, you have a bigger picture."

Ignoring his quiet comment, I continued, "I thought I understood all about the lesson stuff. What boggles my mind is how I messed up so badly after everything I've learned. This shouldn't be happening to me."

George looked me straight in the eye. "Wait a minute, Partner. Let's talk about what you've done right. You found a career you are passionate about and expanded your business."

"Yes. I love the inspirational speaking ... so ..."

"And you have a comfortable home."

I nodded. Under my breath, I mumbled, "I hope."

"And let's not forget about your cat," George chuckled. "You idolize that cat."

I grappled with what he was saying. Didn't he understand I could lose the house and my business? "George, I screwed up. That's why I'm so upset. I stupidly put Matt on the deed to my house, and now I have to pay a small fortune to buy him out. Then my marketing director posted imaginary bookings, so my business is in shambles."

"Oh, I see. I didn't realize that things were that bad." George thought for a moment, then recalled, "You've been in tight spots before; remember when you were living in Los Angeles and you told me you didn't have enough money for rent."

"That happened more often than I care to remember," I said, reflecting on those very lean days. "I would buy plants and pictures on credit, and then canvass office buildings to sell them for profit. By the end of the day I had enough money to pay for the merchandise and my rent." I folded my arms tightly in front of me. "But I don't think you understand. This is different. It's going to take more than selling plants and pictures to get me out of debt this time. I'm in serious trouble."

"The only thing that's different is your attitude or lack of it."

I grumbled, "Why did this happen to me?"

He squinted and I saw something flicker far back in his eyes. I knew he was reaching deep inside for his supply of practical knowledge. He finally asked, "What are your fears? What's blocking you? When you understand your fears, you'll know why this has happened to you."

I shifted uneasily, fumbling for words, because I didn't really want to face my fears. At the same time, if George was to help me, I had to be honest. "I hate admitting this," I finally said. "I ... I'm afraid no man will ever love me, or marry me. I want a family. The man I believed would give me those things left me for a younger woman. I was so desperate to have a man I put him on the deed and now it's costing me a fortune to buy him out. He stole my pride and punched holes in my confidence. He duped me."

"You let this man steal your power, Donna. You knowingly gave it to him. That's a major lesson."

I shook my head. "Why did it have to be so painful?"

George turned his thoughtful eyes on me. "Every soul on the planet has painful lessons to learn. Your insecurities controlled you. You grabbed onto a man, not because he was a wonderful person and treated you well, but because you were needy. You stayed in that relationship because you were afraid to leave and thought no one else would want you. You were willing to settle for an unhappy life. I bet your gut was telling you to get out."

I nodded my head, remembering many intuitive flashes. "You're so right, but I didn't want to listen. My deepest fears are having no man, money, or child. How do I get a handle on them? I don't want my fears controlling me."

George pulled out his pipe and began filling it with tobacco. "The good news is this man will be the last of the worst men in your life. He was the essence of all the men in your past who have disappointed you. Now you can beat this pattern and never repeat it." He reached into his pocket and held out a pen. "Turn over your napkin, take the pen, and write his name on the left side and yours on the right." Reluctantly, I did as he asked. "Now, write down your three most important values."

I sagged back in my chair recalling when George had me write this list once before. I wrote down love, family, and work, in that order.

"Okay. Now, write down what you believe his values were."

Not having to think long, I wrote freedom, fun, and sex.

George noted, "Not one item in common. When your values don't match, you're in conflict. Tell me the truth. If this man came back and asked you to marry him, would you say yes?"

He had asked the one question I didn't want to confront. Would I? Was I that desperate?

"I honestly thought I loved him, and yet it wasn't a loving relationship. We fulfilled each other's 'to-do' lists." I stared down at my napkin and slowly drew in my breath. "No, I wouldn't marry him."

With a grave nod George asked, "How long have you known that? At what moment did your inner voice tell you he wasn't the right man for you?"

My mind searched back to when Matt came into my life. "I guess about two years after we met. When the fun wore thin and he wouldn't talk about marriage or having a family."

"There you go—now that's real honesty. You have to first honor yourself and what you want in your life."

You can't manipulate love
it has to flow naturally

"The men in your past, and yes, Matt too, were there to help illustrate your need to learn to love yourself. Today, you understand that it's common values that support a relationship, not common interest."

"It all makes sense when you explain it, but I couldn't accept it at the time."

"Say, I'm hungry," he said, reaching for a menu. "Can we order dinner now?"

His tone caught me so off guard, I chuckled. He seemed to say, if you don't let me eat now, I'm going to pass out. "Oh, sure. But I don't know about me eating. I have tons more to tell you."

He gave me one of his knowing looks and said, "All right, I'll eat; you talk."

While we waited for the food, I gave George more details of what happened with my marketing director. Indignantly I asked, "How could she steal from me? I trusted her. She had the key to my office and house. She made me feel like she was a friend."

George swallowed a forkful of tamale and said, "She sensed your fear and she saw that you were weak from dealing with Matt. You were in a vulnerable state and your insecurities made it appear that you weren't smart enough to run your own business."

I looked down and fiddled with my hands in my lap.

"I know what you're thinking; you could have done without the boyfriend and the employee fiasco. You attracted those situations so you could gain knowledge. Good! You faced two of your greatest fears at the same time. First, you needed a man. Second, you were not intelligent enough to manage your business."

"You think that's good," I said. "I think it's bad." As I said that, the lesson echoed in my mind. *Stop looking at problems as bad—see them as learning lessons.*

George repeated, "What's good is that you faced them."

I sat up straight and asked, "Is it over?"

With cherry smoke coming out of his pipe, he nodded.

"I'm glad it's over and I'm never going to repeat those lessons again."

George pulled the pipe from his mouth. "Boy, I've been waiting years to hear that. You are finally claiming your own power and doing what's best for your highest good."

I smiled. "I'm a slow learner, but I'm finally getting it."

I got extremely quiet. His words triggered a strong feeling of awareness. The next question popped out unexpectedly. "George, how long have you been looking after me? I don't mean back when I first met you in Hawaii. I mean, even before then."

"Did that question come from you?" he asked.

"Well, no ... yes ... I actually didn't think before talking. It sort of materialized."

"In that case, it's time for you to know," he began as a distant gaze appeared in his eyes. "Call it what you want; I'm your wise man, mentor, or angel. Some people, like you, need a little extra help. I first became aware of you when you were six years old and in the hospital with malnutrition. I sent you some life force to stay alive. You needed some added energy so you could live. After that, I kept checking in on you. There are all kinds of ways to do that. You might say I've done my homework." He chuckled. "And then some."

I hadn't realized my mouth was hanging open until I closed it. "You mean like ESP?"

"Kind of; I've spent years meditating and developing my spiritual knowing," George said. "I was with you again during your heart catheterization at sixteen when you almost died. I sent you some energy to stay alive then too."

I sat in a stupor. "You were there?"

"Yes, in a way. We all have the potential to develop our awareness, but most people are too consumed by their daily experiences to make their spiritual quest a priority." With a twinkle in his eye, he continued, "Including you, there are twelve souls who I look after. I have to say, you're more trouble than all the other eleven put together. None of the others have your stamina, or your questions. You're a real pistol."

I swallowed hard. "Are you saying you've been with me since I was six years old? You watch over me? You were sent by a power greater than both of us?" I stared at him, babbling, "You ... you were ... you ..."

He grinned. "Are you actually at a loss for words? That doesn't happen often."

The waiter arrived to remove the plates and he continued, "I'll have a cup of high-octane coffee and the young lady—give her the unleaded kind." After the waiter left, George said, "Caffeine, right now, would put you right over the top."

He became extremely serious. "You've done a real good job. Now, I want to tell you something and I need you to listen closely. I'll always be with you ... always. All you have to do to connect with me is quiet your mind, say my name, and think about me. You'll feel an awareness that I'm with you. Trust it."

"George, you're so serious. I don't think I have that gift."

"Didn't you have nightmares about the plane crash before it happened?"

I nodded. "But I didn't listen to them."

He ignored what I said, took a minute to light his pipe, and went on talking. "Didn't you have a sense about your cat, Sheba? Exactly what she would look like and that she was coming to you?"

I hesitated. "Yes."

"You have the gift," George said in a tone I had never heard him use before. "You don't know it yet or trust it. My job is to guide you along your spiritual path. I can help you become more aware, but not give you the answers. You'll have to go through the experience of learning certain lessons during this lifetime. I can help you interpret and understand those lessons after the fact, but can't spare the trials or pain of going through them. My role is to provide guidance so you find your way. What I can tell you is that there are three major turning points in your lifetime. If you survive them all, you will be destined to help others."

"Oh my god, the plane crash—that was one, wasn't it?"

"Yes, surviving the crash started you on your journey," he said solemnly.

"If walking through fire was the beginning, then I'm scared to think what could be next. Will the others be so intense? I ... I ... don't know ..." I stammered.

"There's no need to worry; live in the present."

I interrupted him, asking, "But how will I know?"

"Without a doubt, you'll know. Let's you and I go for a walk."

Reluctantly, I closed my mouth and followed him.

George seemed to know right where he was headed. I followed him to a path behind the restaurant where a delightful stream trickled along one side of an embankment. Beautiful mansions sat majestically perched along the banks, with perfectly manicured yards. In the distance was a grove of lush green trees.

We strolled in silence while he smoked his pipe and I smelled the scent of his cherry tobacco. After a while he said, "Don't ever give up on your dreams. Recall what I said about so many people living in pain and disappointment. You can help them, because through your experiences you're better able to understand their pain."

Moving slightly ahead of me, he stopped so suddenly I almost ran into him. There were two rabbits on the path, as still as statues. Suddenly the birds were silent. The rabbits were staring at George, but weren't afraid. There seemed to be communication between them. After awhile, George nodded his head. The rabbits hopped away and the birds resumed their chirping.

"I've never seen you do that before."

He chuckled. "I was having a little after-dinner conversation with my pals."

"But there was no sound."

"I gave you an illustration of what we were talking about earlier. It's a form of telepathy; a way to quietly commune by stilling your mind and focusing your attention. Now with the rabbits, they sensed my calmness and responded."

"Most people talk aloud to animals. They don't do what you did,"

I pointed out.

"Because they believe they can't. Animals and humans silently communicate with us all the time. We don't listen. Don't you talk with Sheba?" he asked.

"Yes, but I have, you know, a little dialogue."

George shrugged, pronouncing, "If I stood here talking to the animals, people would think I was nuts."

Letting out a spontaneous laugh I said, "You know, now that you mention it, George, once when I had a high fever Sheba climbed on my chest and stayed there until the fever broke. She actually helped me get better." I thought for a moment and continued, "But Sheba and I understand each other."

"All living creatures are connected, but you have to work at communicating with them. Through meditation you can quiet the chatter in your mind and focus your attention."

"Tell me more," I said.

"When you meditate, don't worry about how you're going to pay the mortgage. Meditation helps you connect with your source and clears your mind. When you get intuitive hunches, believe in them; it's your higher self communicating the truth."

"I'm glad I came to Denver," I said. "You've given me so much to think about."

We turned to go back and he said, "Like I keep telling you, life is simple."

"Honestly, I want to raise my level of awareness."

"Sure. I've dealt with many contractors through the years. They have a saying that goes like this—"

"Here comes a Georgeism, right?"

He ignored me and continued, "If you're going to build a skyscraper you have to go deep down to build a strong foundation."

"Am I far enough down?"

He chuckled. "That depends on how high you want to go."

"I get the message. I'm grateful. Every time I've needed your help, you've been there for me. I don't know how to thank you for all you've done."

"All I ask in return is that you lend a guiding hand to others when they need help."

"How will I know how to help them?"

"Like I always say, you'll know when you know. I can't always be with you, and situations will come along when you'll have to trust your feelings. Please work to raise your level of consciousness. I know you have flashes all the time; they may be disconnected or hazy, but pay attention to what they're revealing. Honor them. Some call it a sixth sense; others, intuition. It can come as a fleeting moment that brings a strong feeling or a persistent little voice telling you something. You must believe and act on your intuition."

It seemed as if George was cramming me for a final exam. He had a sense of urgency about him, as if I had to understand everything he was saying. Whatever his reason, I would do my best to comprehend his instruction.

"How will I know my feelings are genuine and not my ego telling me what I want to hear?"

"That's why meditation is important. Quiet your mind of its chatter to raise your awareness. Be receptive to the universal truth. It takes patience and practice, but you're already on your way. Next time we are together, I'll share with you the five levels of intuition. This is the wisdom of the ages. This is what I'm meant to pass on to you. You will learn how to develop your intuition and trust it in all situations."

I giggled. "I can't wait! I'll be counting the days."

"Easy, Partner, everything in due time," George said. "For now, let's head back toward your hotel. It's getting dark, and you'll require a good night's rest if you're going to rise and shine for breakfast at 6:00 AM."

I groaned. "Another early morning breakfast? Just teasing, you're worth it."

As he turned to leave the lobby through the revolving doors, I pulled a little book from my purse. "Wait, George. Wait a minute," I intoned, running to catch up with him. "Could you read this?"

He chuckled. "Sounds important."

"It is. I would like your opinion." I handed him a copy of my newly published little book, *Is Your Attitude Showing?*

George took the book from me and perused the title thoughtfully. "Is that all it takes, an attitude adjustment?"

I laughed, announcing, "I've been working on my attitude for thirty years."

"It doesn't matter how long it takes; thirty years, thirty days, thirty hours, or thirty seconds," he said. "Learning is what it's all about. I'll look it over tonight. I've got a good feeling about it."

True to his word, George arrived at the coffee shop early the next morning. This time we both ate pancakes and afterward, he drove me to the airport. While walking to the gate, he reached into his pocket and handed me back my book. "It's good stuff. This little book will help lots of people. When you get home, be sure to put this lucky copy in a safe place."

When the call came to board my flight, I held George close and didn't want to let go. "Thank you so much." Turning to walk down the jetway, I abruptly stopped to ask, "Hey, this plane isn't going to crash, is it?"

He smiled, answering, "No way, Donna. You can't get off the planet that easy. You still haven't completed your assignment. Now, get happy."

Continuing down the boarding ramp, I turned to wave a final goodbye and heard his familiar voice order, "Get happy!"

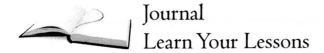

Journal
Learn Your Lessons

Don't complain — create

As usual, George is my saint. A few therapeutic hours with him calmed me down and gave me a new perspective. He has a way of getting me off my merry-go-round and making me look at the core issues. He was right ... where were my values? I thought long and hard and my brain kept churning on the entire plane ride home. These recurring patterns are not serving me. I have to get rid of them once and for all. Gone!

These last few weeks have been extremely difficult. When I get depressed I have zero energy. Starting now, I get to rebuild my life. My energy is already feeling better. Next on my list is an attitude adjustment. Maybe I should reread the book I wrote, *Is Your Attitude Showing?*

Universe, I claim that I have lessons. Can I make a deal? How about they are not so painful next time? I swear I will conquer these waves of unworthiness. Can I swear? Okay journal, at least I have some humor.

I saved the best for last. George. Do I truly comprehend what he said? That he was assigned to take care of me during malnutrition and my heart catheterization? I remember, even at that young age, a surge of energy going through me. WOW, was that really George? How can he do that? Every time I talk to George he makes my problems seem manageable. He has a way of breaking them down and relating them to a lesson. He simplifies the knowledge I must implement. I am thankful he doesn't make me feel stupid for the choices in my life. With kindness he reminds me to meditate and get back on my path.

The important thing is that even if I can't see George or talk to him I can make contact spiritually.

During the plane crash I knew that someone was helping me stay alive and I asked if it was him. He said "No"; it was a greater power than him.

I feel like I am only scratching the surface on my spiritual journey. This is my question. What will George reveal to me when we meet next?

Learning lessons
are a part of life

Chapter Fifteen

Center Your Energy

When you're ready
the opportunity will arise

Browsing in the kitchen cabinets for something to eat, I summarized my choices to be ... rice. Brown, white, wild, or Spanish. Behind the rice lurked a few bags of noodles. Surveying my limited selection, I decided to check the contents of the refrigerator. A swiftly completed inventory included two apples, an orange, mustard, and catsup; so rice it would be.

The seven-day workweek was grueling, but it was starting to pay off. After visiting George in Denver, I landed a sizeable contract with a bank in Southern California. I drove from Tahoe to Los Angeles, talked them into hiring me, slept in my car, and drove home again. In three weeks I would conduct a week of seminars called, "Is Your Attitude Showing?" based on my little book. Still in the process of adjusting my own attitude, here I was teaching techniques to others. Teaching "attitude" guaranteed I would have to live it, breathe it, and do it! I'm sure my mentor would let loose a good belly-laugh at the irony of the situation.

My persistent work ethic was helping me get out of debt. Throughout the year I was speaking all around the United States, and was pleasantly surprised to book international engagements in New Zealand, Australia, and England, landing my first foreign gig when another speaker got sick and cancelled.

I couldn't wait to talk to George after every trip and share my adventures and stories about people I'd met. He would always recount one of his Georgeisms, insisting people were the same the world over. They put on one pant leg at a time. I would accuse him of being an Oakie from Oklahoma and ask what did *he* know? Of course he was right, and he had been telling me that forever. I guess it was finally time for me to listen.

On a personal level, I dated a man from New Zealand who really stole my heart. He was kind and gentle and we had a connection. I felt so at peace when we were together and I could tell him anything. In the long run, it was the distance that wouldn't allow our relationship to grow. He was an amazing man and he made me laugh, but we lived too far apart.

The only way I could survive the disappointment was to throw myself into work with even more commitment. I wasn't the type to pursue the dating scene, so I expected my love life to be on pause. Besides giving speeches I became the host of a weekly television show. Thank heavens my spare time was filling up along with my bank account! After a few weeks of taping, I was assigned a new producer. Jackson was a calming factor when I would get frustrated because the show wasn't going the way it should. He saw me at my best and also at my worst. After a few weeks, he surprised me by asking me out. I was dating someone who liked his work. At least we had one common value.

Sure I was the owner of my own business, but I was also the head janitor. Every Thursday I would complain as I pushed and pulled my garbage cans up and down my long driveway. When it was icy wintertime in the Sierras, I found myself on my butt, with a trash can for a lousy buoy, more often than I cared to remember. So much for the graceful ice skater I used to be. I would complain to Jackson, "The day I can afford garbage cans with rollers is the day I will consider myself rich." There was always something else to buy for the business instead of new cans. Hey, let's not be wasteful; I did have two cans that worked. On Christmas morning there were two large garbage cans with rollers, tied together by a big red bow, sitting next to the tree with a card that read, "Magic happens. You're rich! Jackson."

We worked together and dated for years. Then it was time for the conversation about our future. We enjoyed each other's company and had a lot in common. Two points for the positive. He was adamant that he did not want to be married or have children. Two strikes for the negative. I reluctantly came to terms with what he was saying. I was smarter this time, and I didn't hope or try to change him. We remained good friends. So maybe I was getting wiser.

I still felt angry whenever I saw my ex, Matt, in our resort town with his girlfriend, now his wife. To add insult to injury, I was still making monthly payments to him. He had moved on with his life and he had bought a new, big house. When I complained to George, he retorted with a Georgeism, "It's not good or bad, it's your learning lesson."

Most of the time, I was positive in my outlook. I figured it was the right time for my mentor to pass on the wisdom of the ages. I understood the basics, but wasn't confident enough to know how I could I really help others. Finally, after many conversations he instructed me that there were two areas of my life that needed to be addressed. First, clean up my relationships with my mother, father, and brother. He assured me that it was possible to heal with them. Throughout my life, their inability to express their love made me feel unworthy and unlovable. This led to my pattern of unhealthy relationships with men starting in my teens and carrying forward into my adult life. Did I think that having my senior prom date leave me during prom night for another girl was an indication of things to come? George was adamant that clearing these negative experiences, whether real or imagined, would afford me more energy to develop my intuitive abilities.

The second issue I needed to address was my lack of confidence. There were times when I felt self-assured; then challenges would arise that would send me back into self-doubt, and my negative patterns would sabotage me. This cyclical pattern of taking two steps forward and one step back was exhausting my energy.

Even though George was insistent I work on these issues, he was careful to tell me that I didn't need to resolve them completely before learning the gift of intuition. But I always had to be aware of how they could cause manic emotional swings in my behavior and outflank my best intentions to achieve my highest purpose.

When a flier arrived in the mail for an upcoming seminar on personal power, the timing couldn't have been better. I literally tingled while reading the description: "Forgive your past, face your fears, and break out of negative patterns once and for all. Design your destiny and live your dreams."

Friends told me this seminar was an absolute "must" and that I would actually "walk across hot coals." Heck, I could do that, I told myself. After all, hadn't I walked through fire in the plane crash? Here was an opportunity to release my negative patterns and develop tools to empower myself. Between payments to Matt, the house, and business expenses, I had no extra money. A couple of days later, a girlfriend called to inform me she had a free ticket for the seminar and asked if I would want to go. I guess George would call this a sign; I was meant to go.

Two weeks later in San Jose, California, I stood in line with hundreds of others waiting to participate in the course. Once inside the convention center, I felt energy so powerful it could have lit up half the city. When Tony Robbins appeared on stage, a tumultuous roar of applause and stomping feet reverberated throughout the center. Expectation and hope radiated from the crowd of eager faces.

My plan was to find a good seat, take lots of notes, and gain enough knowledge to heal the dents in my self-esteem. As eager as I was to remedy my life, I wasn't prepared for the intense emotional release that consumed me when I began taking inventory.

The leader instructed us to close our eyes as we were led through a series of probing questions about our pasts. Within minutes I was reliving the agony of betrayal, hopelessness, and neediness that had plagued me. Violence, criticism, and disinterest came flooding back.

I mumbled, "If more misery lies ahead, I don't want to live." Silent tears became deeps sobs that racked my body. Others around me were weeping as well, and soon the auditorium was awash in tears.

In the midst of this emotional turmoil we were asked to refocus our thoughts to the present and begin the steps to reprogram our lives.

The leader said, "When you release the pain of the past, you create the space to design your future."

George had been telling me about my need to work through the past. This emotional purging created the ability to open up my life to new experiences.

With the promise of a renewed spirit, we were guided through the visualization of our desires. "Envision your ideal life for the next month, then a year and two years."

Sitting there, seeing nothing, I waited for something to occur to me. I fidgeted in my seat, and waited, and waited. Then suddenly, a vision ... an expansive stage, applause. There were glimpses of ... I furrowed my forehead and massaged the side of my temples. Could it be ...?

A commanding voice jarred me from my reverie, instructing, "Return to the present and lock your visions into memory."

Armed with the desire to manifest our destiny, we began to prepare for the firewalk finale. We spent the next hour being super-charged with positive chants and affirmations. Cheering, we walked outside toward the beds of red-hot coals arranged on the ground, glowing like a sea of crimson plankton. Coaches instructed us to line up before the burning embers. My senses were heightened. The four probing questions from the plane crash came back to me ...

Do you love yourself?
Do you have a good relationship
with your family and friends?
Are you living your goals and dreams?
If you die today, have you left this
planet a better place for being here?

It had been far too long since I had asked myself those questions. But today, as I waited to face the fire again, the words exploded through my head. Though I was working on answering "yes" to all four questions, my current thought was comparable to the old adage "Not etched in stone, but scrawled in sand."

A hand touched my shoulder and jolted me back to the present. It was my turn. I adjusted my shoulders while chanting inwardly, *I am unique, I am about to experience life to the fullest.* The two guides asked if I was ready to fire-walk and I replied, "Yes. I am ready."

A chilling spray of water on my feet confirmed that I had indeed prevailed over fire. I turned and examined the scene behind me. Yes, those coals were still smoldering bright red.

As I moved aside, I was totally unprepared for what happened next: a brief vision of something comforting, but so fleeting that I squinted my eyes, attempting to hold on to the image. *Wait! Don't go.*

Journal
Center Your Energy

Life is energy

Why does life have so many ups and downs? Why, when you meet a certain person, is there an instant connection? Why do people fall out of love? Why are there accidents? The firewalk had me questioning everything. So many mysteries beyond what I could rationalize. There is a universal truth—of that, I am sure. My goal is to become one with truth and be in the flow.

My assignment during the plane crash was to help people help themselves. Does everyone have a mission? I believe each one of us has value and a purpose, but whether we choose to fulfill it or not is up to us.

I'm randomly going off topic and writing whatever comes to mind. What if I would have stayed in Pennsylvania where I was born? *Dead.* If I had stayed in Montana? *Frustrated.* How about if I was still living in Hawaii? *Laid-back.* The big question is, What if I was in Los Angeles chasing my dream of being an actress? *Dead.*

WHOA, this is eye opening when I look at my life honestly. I am in the place I'm supposed to be now, in Tahoe. I am blessed to travel and talk to people, and then I get to come home to my mountain town and recharge my spirit.

The second thing that was revealed to me during the plane accident was that late in life I would have a daughter who would grow to be a leader. Any day now. "Late" to me was thirty-five, latest was thirty-nine, but that has come and gone and then some.

George talked to me about making my dreams come true. If plans A, B, and C didn't work, then go to plan Q, R, and S, as long as I wasn't forcing a needy wish of my own upon others. Marriage was conspicuously absent from my horizon, and my age would impose extra risks if I attempted to carry a child. So my strategy is to investigate adoption agencies, fill out the paperwork, and interview with prospective birth parents. Will it happen?

Thank you also to the man upstairs, as George would call you, for being there for me.

I am thankful for the firewalk. It reminded me how precious life is, and that everything is possible when you BELIEVE.

Chapter Sixteen

What Is in a Dream?

When you least expect it
love arrives

New Year's Eve, sitting alone in my home; good going, Donna. I had worked nonstop throughout the entire year and straight through the holiday season without a break. Several times in recent days, I found myself reaching for the phone to call George, but invariably hesitated and pulled back. After all, hadn't I attended the firewalk seminar to become my own person? Though I knew George would always be there for me, part of the growth process was learning how not to sweat the small stuff.

"Happy New Year," I told myself, slathering mustard on my turkey and cheese sandwich. I paused to glance at a box sitting on the edge of the counter. It contained an adorable baby blanket embellished with playful jungle animals. I bought the blanket a few weeks ago to be a visual reminder that a child was in my future. Just as my creative financing and visualization techniques helped to secure the house of my dreams, the blanket was a tool I would use to manifest my daughter.

Meow, I heard, followed by a soft rustle at my feet. There she was.

"Sheba, we're not hungry again!"

Her bright blue eyes opened wide, as if to say, *Speak for yourself—I'm hungry.*

Knowing who was really in charge of this household, I cut up some fresh turkey and put it in Sheba's bowl. Then I decided that a nice warm shower would do me good. My faithful cat made tracks for the living room because her intuition instructed her to be suspicious of spraying water. She never ventured within three feet of a running faucet.

Standing beneath the water stream whittled away my tension. I did some of my best thinking in the shower. An image of the tiny, perfect baby bloomed in my mind. I had talked to a half dozen adoption agencies, all of whom advised that "Birth parents typically pick someone younger, and prefer a husband and wife as adoptive parents." That was their polite way of telling me that a single woman in her forties would not make the top of the list.

Why am I being shut out? Why can't I adopt a child? I paused for a moment, realizing I was letting other people tell me what I should or shouldn't do. I screamed, "No, I'm not giving up on my dream."

I imagined myself in my fifties, then my sixties, alone, with no hope of a child. At that moment, overcome with emotion, I crouched down in the shower, streaming water mingling with tears circling the drain. Pleading, "Please, give me someone to love," while pounding on the tiles, I realized that I may have walked through fire but the fire in my heart was fueled by fear of loneliness.

Shivering violently, I finally noticed that the hot water had run out. Raising my head, I saw a small form outside the shower door. To my amazement, Sheba was clawing at the door, trying to open it with her paw.

The door clicked open. I unclenched my hands and stared at her in disbelief. Sheba had one paw on the step and her head in the shower, her blue eyes wide with terror. For an instant, time stood still. Then, hesitantly, she put both front paws into the water. After another moment of indecision, Sheba had all four paws in the shower. My cat, who was terrified of running water, had conquered her fear so she could come to me. Unbelievable. She loved me so much, she ventured into the very thing she feared most.

Despite my despair, I chuckled. Queen Sheba, my beautiful white Himalayan, was standing in the shower looking every bit the wet alley cat. Cocking her head, she began meowing plaintively as if to say, *Let's get out of here. Now!*

My sweet little cat was teaching me to love and overcome my fears.

Teeth chattering, I turned off the water, picked up Sheba, and wrapped towels around us both. Then, laughing through tears of joy, I acknowledged that I had at least one healthy relationship; sure, it was with a cat, but at least I had one. Sheba showed me the healing power of love.

Drying her off, I looked into her eyes and read, *Look Mom, I know how badly you want a kid. Do a good job raising me, a four-legged kid. Then your next adventure will be with a two-legged one.* Something inside of me shifted right then, and I felt inexplicably different and better.

An hour later in bed, I propped up my pillows, feeling a strong urge to meditate. Emptying my mind of doubt and opening myself to all possibilities, I entered a state of total relaxation and vaguely glimpsed an image of a pink blanket.

Shaken out of my state of meditation, I recalled George telling me that our intuition is there to guide us, and that we can develop it to gain insight into what our future holds. My dreams had given me the knowledge about the plane crash but I chose to ignore them. *Is what I'm seeing in my mind now true? Is it my daughter? Or is my mind playing tricks?*

George had explained that the higher you lifted your spiritual vibration, the more "in the flow" you became and the more your life would unfold naturally. "Your lessons are there to teach you—to give you inner wisdom," he would say.

My retort to him was always the same. "If I go through any more lessons I'll be so strong I won't need a door; I'll just walk right through the wall."

He'd throw up his hands and say, "Your past has taught you, but your future will be extraordinary."

Through my trials I have come to understand the importance of persistence. I am now resolved to manifest one more assignment that was given to me in the plane crash: having a daughter. My adoption plans would remain in motion, even though friends looked at me strangely, some offering patient smiles normally reserved for the senile. Some explained gently that I was a bit too old to raise an infant, and shouldn't be disappointed if the adoption didn't happen. I told them all the same thing. "I will never give up!"

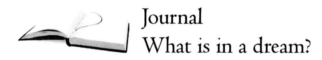 Journal
What is in a dream?

There are no accidents
Everything happens for a reason

The plane crash altered who I am. I look at life differently. It took a horrific tragedy to open my eyes to the possibilities that each day holds.

I had not appreciated what I was given. Moments before the accident I said, "Let my life change. Let it never be the same. Or let me die." I begged for change; now I am going to live it. The uncertainty that change brings is frightening. My task is to embrace change and accept it. My goal is to be in the flow, even if that means moving out of my comfort zone. I know if I'm to develop wisdom, CHANGE IS FOR MY HIGHTEST GOOD.

When the student is ready, the teacher appears. When I develop a higher vibration my mentor, the seventh son of a seventh son, will bestow on me his knowledge of intuition. With this wisdom I can focus on making decisions for my highest good during challenging times. I crave this KNOWING.

Universe, thank you for providing me with firepower. I am determined to make my dreams come true.

Like souls come together
when the time is right

Fire Up Series

In these uncertain times, the human spirit yearns for hope and enlightenment so each of us may survive and thrive. The **Fire Up** series recounts a compelling true-life journey, delivering timely inspiration along with timeless wisdom. Donna Hartley is crowned Miss Hawaii and her attention is captured by a kind and patient soul, George, who mysteriously prophesies that her success is paved with learning lessons. He relates to her in storytelling form that Donna must survive three life-threatening events if she is to fulfill her destiny. Is George a wise man, a mentor, an angel, or all three?

Fire Up Your Life! recounts Donna's near-death experience in a DC-10 plane crash at Los Angeles International Airport, which occurs directly after she expresses her desire to change her life or die. Trapped in the flaming inferno, she receives a mysterious message questioning her actions on earth. She wills herself to survive and is the last passenger out of her section of the aircraft. With the steadfast help of her teacher George, the reluctant student Donna begins a journey of spiritual transformation committing herself to change her fearful and unhealthy lifestyle. Her first assignment is to fight for improved airline safety regulations. Next, she must conquer her destructive relationships with men. Moreover, to become a successful entrepreneur she must master her fears.

Fire Up Your Intuition! finds Donna distraught in an emotional and financial crisis. George unexpectedly appears and bestows on her five mysterious envelopes that hold a 30-day assignment that he calls "the gift of intuition." The banter and discussion continue between student and teacher as Donna works to acquire insight into her own intuitive awareness. Her faithful Himalayan cat Sheba is by her side as Donna follows George's program step by step to learn to trust her feelings and act upon them to master *the knowing*. George predicts that when she completes her assignment, her dream to adopt a daughter will come true.

Fire Up Your Healing! narrates the sometimes rocky path on the passage toward family forgiveness leading to emotional maturity and the strength to heal. Donna travels from the tragic confines of her mother's post-stroke nursing home to the somber quarters of the judge empowered with deciding the fate for the bitter court battle in which her stepmother has embroiled Donna and her brother upon their father's death. George adamantly advises her to release her anger in order to survive. Could she forgive the alcoholism, the violence, and the indifference? This skill is now essential if she is to survive her stage III melanoma. But can she forgive herself and live to raise her six-year-old daughter? George mystically appears in the hospital to give Donna a shot of spiritual adrenalin and the courage to face down the deadly disease.

Fire Up Your Heart! begins at the gravesite of her stepdad as a heartbroken Donna deals with the eleventh death of family and friends in the past few years. Her nagging intuition forces her to consult a heart specialist and the prognosis is her worst fear: she must have immediate open-heart surgery to replace her failing aortic valve. Her daughter Mariah, now age ten, is the driving force to help her live. Donna's friends rally to lend her support for the delicate surgery scheduled for **March 1**, the same date of her plane crash and melanoma diagnosis. What are those chances? Donna must summon all her strength and hard-won wisdom to survive. Will George spiritually guide her through this life-threatening operation? Has Donna learned her lessons so she can cheat death for the third time?

CPSIA information can be obtained
at www.ICGtesting.com
Printed in the USA
FSOW01n0616200117
29807FS